JOHN KOBAL PRESENTS THE

T·O·P

100

MOVIES

A PLUME BOOK

NEW AMERICAN LIBRARY

NEW YORK AND SCARBOROUGH, ONTARIO

EDITOR: John Kobal

RESEARCH: Peter Cargin

Dedicated to the memory of Carlos Clarens
(1930-1987) whose love of movies was a gift
which he knew how to share with all his friends,
and in memory of all the lists of our favourites
which we would draw up on those long London
nights with only Jeanette's *Merry Widow* and
Irene Dunne's *Roberta* for company.
Here's thinking of you, Carlos.

NAL BOOKS ARE AVAILABLE AT QUANTITY DISCOUNTS WHEN USED TO
PROMOTE PRODUCTS OR SERVICES. FOR INFORMATION PLEASE WRITE
TO PREMIUM MARKETING DIVISION, NEW AMERICAN LIBRARY,
1633 BROADWAY, NEW YORK, NEW YORK 10019.

First published in Great Britain in 1988 by PAVILION BOOKS LIMITED
196 Shaftesbury Avenue, London WC2H 8JL in association with
Michael Joseph Limited, 27 Wrights Lane, Kensington, London W8 5TZ

Published by arrangement with Pavilion Books Limited.

 PLUME TRADEMARK REG U.S. PAT OFF. AND FOREIGN COUNTRIES
REGISTERED TRADEMARK–MARCA REGISTRADA
HECHO EN HARRISONBURG, VA., U.S.A.

SIGNET, SIGNET CLASSIC, MENTOR, ONYX, PLUME, MERIDIAN and
NAL BOOKS
are published *in the United States* by NAL PENGUIN INC.,
1633 Broadway, New York, New York 10019, and *in Canada* by
The New American Library of Canada Limited, 81 Mack Avenue,
Scarborough, Ontario, M1L 1M8.

LIBRARY OF CONGRESS
Library of Congress Cataloguing-in-Publication Data

John Kobal presents the top 100 movies
p.   cm.
ISBN 0-452-26146-5
1. Motion pictures – Evaluation. 2. Motion pictures – History and
criticism. I. Kobal, John. II. Title: Top 100 movies.
PN1995.9.E9J54 1988
791.43'75 – dc19   88–15582
CIP

Designed by Bridgewater Design

First Plume Printing, October, 1988

1   2   3   4   5   6   7   8   9

Printed and bound in Great Britain

AUTHOR'S NOTE

In the first place I am indebted to the critics,
writers and film-makers who took time out of
their hectic schedules to play this game with
me; to Stuart Spencer in New York, who took
time out from his writing to organize much of
this material for me; to Dave Kent for his
manifold contribution correcting errors, getting
credits and finding the pictures and, of course,
to Peter Cargin for doing that amazing research
without which I don't wish to think of what I
would be doing now.

THE TOP 100: AN ALPHABETICAL LISTING

INTRODUCTION

Who would have thought that working on this book would prove fun? Not I. Even though, over a very pleasant lunch, I must have said 'yes' to the idea. 'Yes' is so easy over a lunch with wine. The trouble with deals signed with pens dipped in wine is that they leave you with a headache the morning after and a job that won't go away. How pleasant to find I was enjoying my work once I got down to reading those quirky, amusing, illuminating and always personal observations from the men and women who worked on the films that had become part of all of our lives. Half-way through the notes which my colleague Peter Cargin provided on *Viaggio in Italia*, I felt, rumbling in my stomach, an overwhelming desire to see the film. The Rossellini sounded so wonderful. There was poor George Sanders, the film's male lead, coming to his co-star Ingrid Bergman in tears of frustration over her husband's methods of making films. Her philosophical assurance, 'Well, Roberto must know what he's doing', after she had spent several days being filmed in a museum in Naples looking at statues, didn't lift his gloom. This Neopolitan approach to making a movie about 'estrangement' left the Anglo-Russian George so estranged from everything Italian (and Swedish) that he put a long-distance call through to his 'estranged' Hungarian wife Zsa Zsa, who delayed becoming a Prince's bride to return and comfort her soon-to-be ex-husband. It was a scenario worthy of the Spanish director Buñuel.

Of course the film was wonderful. Of course Ingrid was right to keep her faith in her husband when all about her were losing theirs. Rossellini was at the helm and whatever the outcome, having already left home, fame, one family and a secure fortune to start her career anew as Roberto's mistress, muse and the mother of his children, she wisely went along. Her reward was a magnificent body of films that few went to see at the time but which we appreciate and admire today for the fresh perspective they brought to film making. *Viaggio* was like some Jungian journey without which we might never have had Antonioni's *L'Avventura* or Resnais' *L'Anneé Dernière à Marienbad*.

Peter had found many such wonderful bits of information: Kurosawa on Ford, Ford on Wayne, Wayne on Hawks, Hawks on *Casablanca*; Ingrid Bergman, Francesco Rosi, Federico Fellini *and* George Sanders about Rossellini; Ingmar Bergman about Tarkovsky; Tarkovsky about his childhood . . . Marvellous memories.

But, at the same time, so many hardships to create these films. Time and again one reads of the difficulties so many of these artists had while making these films or getting them distributed and seen by the public: *Greed* was cut and cut and cut again before it was at last released in its mutilated form; through most of the production the stars of *Casablanca* didn't know how their story would end. William Randolph Hearst used the full power of his press to try and stop the distribution of *Kane*; *La Règle du Jeu*, *Freaks* and *Zéro de Conduite* had to wait decades before they were finally seen by the general public. The Japanese director Mizoguchi was at his lowest ebb when he made his masterpiece, *Life of O-Haru*; Jean Vigo was dying when he made *L'Atalante*; Chaplin suffered persecution by the media during *Monsieur Verdoux*; Eisenstein was never able to complete the third part of hi... posed *Ivan* trilogy, and died long before the second part was permit... seen; John Ford fared little better with Zanuck than Eisenstein had with Stalin, and after what Zanuck did to *My Darling Clementine*, Ford left Fox, after twenty-five years.

The space allowed – 250 words per film – seem a lot before you start but far too little once you get down to what you love – meant that only so much could be used. But enough, I hope, to make you wish to read more, and to see the films to which they are witness: not only the familiar, the classics, the ones now taught in classes, the ones that are the staples of film societies and television, but the others, long heard of but rarely seen, revered but forgotten, and now brought suddenly to life again through an Ozu's memory, a Rosi's insight, a Fellini's throw-away observation, or an actor's comical 'despair'.

The 100 that eventually made up *the* final 100 had nothing to do with me.

Don't understand these things. Never have. Don't want to. To pick one's ten best, ten favourites, ten anything brings on the creeping sickness in me. Paralysis. How can I be sure I won't change my mind? As one whose tastes suffer dramatic changes by the day of the week and by the weather on that day, I've always been in two minds about making up my mind and lean toward Scarlett O'Hara's philosophical attitude when wondering what to do. Like her I believe that, 'Tomorrow *is* another day.'

Still, it was intriguing to see which films were liked. By whom? And why? And to realize how much one's tastes in films are still ruled by geography and age. Clearly, *Citizen Kane*, coming at the top of the list as it has so often before (both in the number of critics who mentioned it and the number of total votes it received), strikes some special response that lifts it above its American roots to appeal equally to women as well as men, the young and the old, the Frenchman and the Russian, the Italian and the Algerian. And yet, though as a director Welles has always had the charismatic appeal of a James Dean, the only other of his films to gain enough votes to make it into this list was *Touch of Evil*, a wonderfully seedy film-noir he made seventeen and seven films after *Kane*.

Assuming that the paucity of American critics, in proportion to that country's size, accounts for the absence of so many 'legendary' American films and their directors in this final tally, by the same token it raises an interesting point which I'd never thought about before, namely, that despite the far-reaching power and global impact enjoyed by the American cinema, without local support many American 'classics' are not regarded in the same light outside the US of A. In this group of 100 films, thirty-nine are American, and three directors – Hitchcock, John Ford and Charlie Chaplin (two of whom were British) – account for almost half of them. Yet in terms of output over the years covered here, Hollywood turned out almost as many films as all the other countries put together (excluding that Hollywood on the Ganges, which for all of its prolific production has only one director, Satyajit Ray, to show on this list). And since the end of the First World War they distributed them over a larger proportion of the earth's surface than any other country has ever been able to do.

From the outset I believed it was vital to have the contributors' ages. This would help to make clear, as previous compilations failed to do, the universal appeal of Renoir's *La Grande Illusion*, Ford's *The Searchers*, von Stroheim's *Greed* and Hitchcock's *The Lady Vanishes*. The older critics had obviously seen these films on their first release and never forgotten them. Others, my generation for example, raised in the backwaters when it came to foreign films, saw them for the first time on TV in the wee small hours when the folks were asleep. In the early 50s, foreign films in my Canadian home were more common on TV than those from Hollywood. Except of course those Lippert, Eagle Lion and Republic masterpieces. (That might partly explain the discovery in the 70s of 40s B-film directors like Edgar G. Ulmer and films like *Detour*!) By the time the Hollywood studios opened their vaults to TV, I had become as familiar with French and Italian films as with the latest Universal-International release. (Of all the major American companies, none had less right to regard the appeal of their product as being either Universal or International.) Even if Silvana Mangano, Anna Magnani, Sophia Loren, Gina Lollobrigida, and Ingrid Bergman all sounded alike (all were dubbed, by the same person – rumour has it it was a *man*), those small-screen late-night showings whetted one's curiosity and planted a growing love for Blasetti, Lattuada and Rossellini.

Other contributors, those under thirty, probably saw many of the old and famous films first as students, shown to them by one of the former, who instilled them with their enthusiasms as well as their prejudices. After which they went away to discover Lynch and Romero and Edgar G. Ulmer, as well as Welles and Kurosawa.

Going through this list one realizes how vital a role the post-War rise of the Cannes and Venice Film Festivals played in introducing the American movie to the European film makers, the West to the East, and silent films to sound. Until Kurosawa's triumph at Venice with *Rashomon* in 1951, hardly anyone in the West had ever seen a Japanese film. Cannes was responsible for launching the reputation of Satyajit Ray and thus creating an interest in more of the Indian cinema. Berlin, set up originally by the Allies to help keep that city artistically alive, has proven to be not only a great bridge with the eastern European film-makers but it established a parallel reputation for its superior retrospectives. Even the less glamorous and high-powered London Film Festival provided the forum that enabled the single-minded Irish cinephile Kevin Brownlow to rescue one of the legends of France's silent cinema from oblivion and re-launch Abel Gance's virtually forgotten *Napoléon* with fully orchestrated splendour to acclaim around the world. Without Brownlow's passionate scholarship and dedication it's doubtful that *Napoléon* would have found its way on to this list.

More recently, if it hadn't been for its 1984 screening at Venice it's a safe guess that the marathon *Heimat* would never have been seen as widely outside its own heimat, and at over fifteen hours in length, not there much either. What Hollywood did for the importance of the STAR, film festivals did for directors and the films of other countries. Through them, films truly became an international medium. Festivals helped to break down the parochial outlook that has always lurked just below the surface and brought back that communication between the people of nations which silent film buffs so loved to tell us had been lost with the coming of sound.

These choices provide other surprises as well. Before any of the replies had come in, I was fairly certain that we would find the inevitable *Kane*, *Rashomon*, *Potemkin*, *Bicycle Thieves*, and *La Grande Illusion*, and that these films would still be leading the list as they have for so many years now. But it seemed as sure as rain in Britain on a Bank Holiday that with a hundred films there would be room somewhere down the line for popular works by Lang, Ford, von Sternberg, Rossellini, Douglas Sirk, Frank Capra, Godard, Fellini and Bergman: idols of the critics.

Recently there had been whole books devoted to films like *The Wizard of Oz*, *It's a Wonderful Life*, *Casablanca*, the making of *The African Queen*, Gance's *Napoléon*, and even *Heaven's Gate*(!) to ensure that when prize-giving time rolled round these films and/or their makers would still be fresh in people's minds. However one arrived at and in whatever order one chose to list one's ten, I felt certain that some of my own personal favourites would find their way into the 100. The Pabst/Brook's *Lulu*, the Mankiewicz/Davis *All About Eve*, the Vidor/Cooper *Fountainhead*, Wilder/Swanson's *Sunset Boulevard* and Sturges/Stanwyck's *The Lady Eve*. At least one Stanwyck film. If not her *Eve*, then one with Wilder or even with Sirk. Just so one could have the chance to hear again her voice brushing the nape of one's neck, that look and that shrug of hers was worth a film in its own right. She wasn't just a great film star but a director's dream. American choices would take care of her, I thought, the way the French were bound to look after Arletty, the Italians their Anna Magnani, and though the Germans might not want to, one hoped that Romy Schneider would steal in on the arm of Visconti, or some such. And I felt sure there would be one of the 30s musicals, hopefully (though not *Top Hat* again!). And why not *Gilda*, that 40s *Lulu*? I couldn't be the only one for whom the gorgeous *Gilda*, more than a lot of better films in that genre, conjures up that whole dim-lit world of noir. Or could I?

My surprise therefore was not with what was in, but with what had been left out. So, OK, no *Gilda*, no *Laura*. Those had always been pipe dreams. But, no films by Frank 'The Name Before The Title' Capra? And none by Preston Sturges? No *Palm Beach Story*, no *Miracle at Morgan's Creek*? No Stanwyck!!! What trough had they fallen into to account for their absence? Sturges, like Lubitsch, would, I felt sure, be strongly represented. But then, there was nothing by D W Griffith, King Vidor, George Cukor, George Stevens. Even the Oscar-rich William Wyler only just slipped in with *Best Years*. Nor were there any films made by that triumverate of American 50s ikons, Nick (*Rebel Without a Cause*) Ray, Samuel (*Pick-up on South Street*) Fuller and Douglas (*Imitation of Life*) Sirk. And, considering the earth-shaking impact which the arrival of the French Nouvelle Vague created in the late 50s, was it possible that the revolutionary work of its leaders, Godard, Chabrol, Louis Malle, would have become as passé as the expressionist German cinema of the 20s? Apparently, yes. Works by some of these directors appear on individual lists but with too few votes to make them count.

The thought then arose, is film the international language it's so often claimed to be (at least as long as you can read the subtitles when you don't understand the language), or is it still based on very parochial considerations? Only a very few films made over the breadth of this century have managed to reach up and out from their own national boundaries to touch the minds and hearts of filmgoers everywhere. Whereas one doesn't have to be French to like Colette's novels, or German to like Strauss's operas or American to like musicals and cowboy stories, when it comes to movies, the dividing lines are much firmer.

Of course, though I tried to stress the sort of films one would love to be cast away with on a desert island, most people took care in compiling their top ten as the ten best films of all time. Quite different from choosing the ten films one liked the best. Ultimately, what this selection reveals, loud and clear, and, dare I say, reassuringly, is a profoundly humanist cinema. If there are stars in it, well and good. But little spectacle, little violence, a little staring into space and looking at statues, but overall, the majority of these films are concerned with people, with their feelings, with their need to communicate with each other. With that as its primary consideration, the film can be made anywhere and reach everyone.

Today, of course, we have a new group of cinephiles, who, through the technology of video, are able to see a wider range of films in a shorter space of time and with greater ease than any generation before. In the early days cinemas were places to which a lot of people could go to see a movie. Today a lot of movies can be seen by individuals in their homes. Cinemas may be dying but movies are alive and well. What we have here, is a tribute to the magic of the cinema and to personal choice. It is a good representation of the 100 best films ever made. Ultimately this list knows no political or social boundaries. And even if many of your personal favourites are missing, this list is an acknowledgement to the art of the cinema.

John Kobal
London, April 1988

PUBLISHERS' NOTE

A panel of film experts from twenty-two countries filled in a questionnaire on which they were invited to list their 'top ten favourite movies of all time' including any film that they felt qualified as a full-length feature. The panellists were also invited to name the first movie they recalled seeing and either their least favourite movie of all time or the first movie they can recall walking out of. Any further comments could be written on the back of the questionnaire.

In compiling the top 100, we awarded 10 points for a number one, 9 points for a number two, 8 points for a number three, and so on. In those cases when an elector chose not to rank the top ten in order, the total number of points available, 55, was divided equally by ten and each movie received 5½ points. In the case of movies that drew the same number of points, they are placed in alphabetical order.

Many of the films have been released under different titles in Britain and the USA, for example *A Matter of Life and Death* (UK) was *Stairway to Heaven* in the USA, and some non-English language films are known only by their original title – ie *Jules et Jim*. We have listed films under the title most commonly used; translations and/or alternative titles are also given on page 3 and under the film's entry.

1 CITIZEN KANE

The impact of *Citizen Kane* is beyond dispute. It is a film that begs for superlatives and, for the most part, it gets them. By the time of its release, when Welles was still a trim *enfant terrible* of 26, he already had a full career behind him. A painter, journalist, actor (in Dublin), he had published his own edition of Shakespeare at the age of 19. At 21 he was director of the Negro People's Theatre, creating a sensational all-black production of *Macbeth*. When he was 22 he established the Mercury Theatre where he acted and directed. He also produced radio drama and his production of *War of the Worlds* precipitated the now legendary panic when thousands of listeners took the realistic broadcast for the real thing.

His arrival in Hollywood was preceded by his announcement that he intended to 'create disturbance in the industry'. This he did and more. Yet he denied the accusation levelled at *Citizen Kane*: that it was an exposé of the life of William Randolph Hearst. Welles said, 'I didn't make a picture about him. Hearst was raised by his mother. He had a very happy childhood. My man Kane was raised by a bank. That's the whole point of the picture. They were different types of men.'

Nevertheless, Louella Parsons, having seen only the unfinished picture, reported to Hearst that it was an unauthorized biography of him, and Hearst believed it. The enormous influence he wielded would come to take its toll on Welles' career. Louis B. Mayer went so far as to offer RKO $800,000 for the negative of *Kane*, so that he could destroy it. George Schaefer, head of RKO, turned Mayer down saying, 'Kane is an important film and we are proud of it.' Joseph Cotten, one of the stars of *Kane*, noted that for years after, when a Hearst newspaper reviewed one of his films, even if Cotten were the star, the critic would resolutely fail to mention his name.

The film was from a script by Herman J. Mankiewicz, who had entitled the first draft *America*. The third and final draft, now co-written and retitled by Welles, was dated 16 July 1940 and ran 156 pages long (a standard length is about 110). In addition to this indulgence the studio allowed Welles complete control over his film, including the all-important final cut.

Welles himself received only one Oscar for the film, and that was shared with Mankiewicz for the screenplay.

The impact of *Kane* is difficult to exaggerate. Welles' techniques of dialogue, camera, sound, dramatic structure have all proved enormously influential and durable. The deep focus technique allowed Welles to change the conventional narrative style, and his dispensation of a chronological, linear story allowed him to reconstruct his character like a jigsaw puzzle, through the subjectivity of the various people who had known him.

Directors as diverse as Truffaut, Fellini, Ophuls and Melville have all acknowledged a lasting debt to *Kane*. Truffaut describes the reaction to Welles and his film in Europe, where it was released only in 1946:

Because Welles was young and romantic, his genius seemed closer to us than the talents of the traditional American directors. When Everett Sloane, who plays the character of Bernstein in Kane, *relates how, one day in 1896, his ferryboat crossed the path of another in Hudson Bay on which there was a young woman in a white dress holding a parasol, and that he'd only seen the girl for a second but had thought of her once a month all his life . . . behind this Chekhovian scene, there was no big director to admire, but a friend to discover, an accomplice to love, a person we felt close to in heart and mind.*

The careful, polished surface of the film retains the same enormous power of impact that it possessed on its first opening. Even those who resist naming the 'best' film ever made, will often refer to *Citizen Kane* as, at least, the 'greatest'.

We now look back on *Kane* with a certain sadness, knowing as we do that Welles had reached the pinnacle of his cinematic career with it. He would never achieve the same heights again. 'Time has, ironically, made Welles look a little Kane-ish himself,' commented Isabel Quigley in 1965.

DIRECTOR: Orson Welles

SCREENPLAY: Herman J. Mankiewicz, Orson Welles

PHOTOGRAPHY: Gregg Toland

MUSIC: Bernard Herrmann

LEADING PLAYERS: Joseph Cotten, Dorothy Comingore, Orson Welles, George Coulouris, Agnes Moorehead, Paul Stewart, Ruth Warwick, William Alland, Ray Collings, Everett Sloane

PRODUCTION COMPANY: Mercury Productions

COUNTRY: USA

DATE: 1940

LA RÈGLE DU JEU

THE RULES OF THE GAME

Made on the very eve of the Second World War, when Renoir was working for the first time with complete artistic licence, *La Règle du Jeu*, photographed by his brother, Claude, nevertheless suffered from enormous setbacks, difficulties, misunderstandings, and abuse.

Renoir had the idea of creating a sort of French United Artists, to produce not only his work but that of other directors as well. With help from the government, he set up the operation, and started work on what he referred to as a 'drame gai'. He wanted to expound on the theme he had developed in *La Grande Illusion* – that nobody is completely good or completely bad, that there are always mitigating circumstances for people's behaviour.

His story was taken from Musset's *Les Caprices de Marianne*, though little of the original remains in the finished film. The music of Mozart opens and closes the film, and is introduced with a quotation from *The Marriage of Figaro*. Renoir set his scene at a country house party, and divided the action between the aristocrats upstairs and the servants below.

Upstairs, the most important thing is to maintain decorum, follow the rules of the game, while at the same time finding sensual pleasure in infidelity. Below, the servants follow their passions, becoming entangled in a farcical triangle. Later, Renoir would say, 'During the shooting of the film I was torn between my desire to make a comedy of it and the wish to tell a tragic story. The result of this ambivalence was that film as it is.'

Budgeted at 2.5 million francs, a hefty sum at the time, *La Règle du Jeu* was to be one of the major films of the year. But with only three weeks to go before shooting was scheduled to start, Renoir had yet to begin casting. He used himself in the role of Octave, originally intended for his brother Pierre, thereby reserving the film's most memorable line for himself: 'There's one thing, do you see, that's terrifying in this world, and that is that every man has his reasons.' The Austrian actress, Nora Gregor, cast as the Marquise, was the Princess Stahrenberg, wife of the claimant to the Austrian throne.

Renoir also ended up taking actors entirely wrong for the roles he had written, and so was forced to reconceive characters at the last minute. (One of the alterations would later bring down the wrath of the anti-semitic French public. Marcel Dalio, a well-known Jewish actor, was cast as the Marquis de la Chesnaye, so Renoir provided in the script that the Marquis had a Jewish mother. It was all the proof the anti-semites needed that French society had been contaminated by the Jews.)

Exterior shooting began in February 1939, at the Château de la Ferte-Sainte-Aubin. They had barely begun work when it started to rain and didn't stop for two weeks. Renoir used the time to finish work on the screenplay, but by the time the rain stopped money was already running out. He was able to get an advance based on the success of his most recent film *La Bête Humaine*, and returned to Paris to shoot interiors at the Joinville Studios. He left two assistants behind at the Château to shoot the animal scenes in the rabbit hunt. This sequence took two months to film and Renoir's delegation has given rise to speculation that he actually had little to do with that

DIRECTOR: Jean Renoir

SCREENPLAY: Jean Renoir, Carl Koch, Camille François

PHOTOGRAPHY: Jean Bachelet

MUSIC: Mozart, Saint-Saëns, Johann Strauss

LEADING PLAYERS: Marcel Dalio, Nora Gregor, Jean Renoir, Roland Toutain, Mila Parély, Paulette Dubost, Julien Carette, Gaston Modot, Pierre Magnier

PRODUCTION COMPANY: Nouvelle Edition Française

COUNTRY: France

DATE: 1939

famous, cataclysmic moment in the film. In fact, Renoir had left behind such a detailed shooting script that the rumour can be confidently dismissed.

Renoir's technique was well advanced by this time. He had made 14 films in the previous eight years. He was using the 'deep focus' technique years before Welles was acclaimed for it in *Citizen Kane*. 'The more I work,' Renoir commented, 'the more I abandon confrontations between the two actors neatly set up before the camera; as in a photographer's studio I prefer to place my characters more freely, at different distances from the camera and to make them move. For that I need a great depth of field.'

In the end, *La Règle du Jeu* cost over 5 million francs and was an unmitigated commercial disaster. Even after it was cut from 112 minutes to 100 by distributors hoping to make it more appealing, the chauvinistic French public hated the thought of French aristocrats with Jewish parents and German wives. Five more minutes were cut to make it fit on to a double bill but attempts were made to burn down the cinema where it was screened, and it was finally banned. The Nazis maintained the ban and the Allies destroyed the original negative on a bombing raid. A single copy was discovered after the war and was further cut before being put back into distribution.

Then, about 1960, two enthusiastic Renoir fans who had bought the rights to *La Règle du Jeu*, discovered 200 cans of working material from the film. From these scraps, they restored the film to its original form, missing only a minute of dialogue.

Audiences could see, for the first time in 22 years, Renoir's vision of society and its mores, and a world-wide appreciation of the film began at that moment. Alain Resnais said, upon viewing it the first time,

it is the single most overwhelming experience I have ever had in the cinema. When I came out of the theatre, I remember I just had to sit on the edge of the pavement, I sat there for a good five minutes and then I walked the streets of Paris for a couple of hours. For me everything had been turned upside down. All my ideas about the cinema had been changed.

3 BATTLESHIP POTEMKIN

BRONENSETS POTYOMKIN

Produced in 1925 as a celebration of the 1905 Revolution, *Battleship Potemkin* has become a standard film in every film course around the world. It is the reference point for countless documentary and dramatic films, which pay homage not only to its style and technique but to specific scenes and moments in the film.

Sergei Eisenstein had originally planned a story with a larger scope, but then settled on this particular episode of the *Potemkin* as a means of revealing the entire revolution.

The film uses repetition [he said] from a tiny cellular organism of the battleship to the organism of the entire battleship, from a tiny cellular organism of the fleet to the organism of the entire fleet – thus flies through the theme the revolutionary feeling of brotherhood.

He shot on location, using the Odessa Steps, and the Battleship *Twelve Apostles*, sister ship of the *Potemkin* which by then had been dismantled.

He rehearsed carefully but used mainly non-professionals in the roles. He was efficient and well-organized, as described later by an assistant on the film: 'After each day's filming we rehearsed the next day's scenes before dinner.' Assistants would be placed in charge of a group of actors. Then,

Antonov's group was to walk or run from one point to another, Gomorov's to move across them, and Lyoshin's at an angle established by the camera's position that day. Each person, representing one hundred, walked or ran through the rehearsed mise-en-scene while Eisenstein made corrections in the shooting script.

Rhythm, motion, repetition – they became central to Eisenstein's method on *Potemkin*. In discussing the famous scene on the Odessa Steps, he said, '*Chaotic* movement (of a mass) – into *rhythmic* movement (of the soldiers). One aspect of moving speed (rushing people) – into the next stage of the same theme of moving speed (rolling baby carriage). Movement *downward* – into movement *upward*.'

DIRECTOR:	Sergei Eisenstein
SCREENPLAY:	Sergei Eisenstein
FIRST TREATMENT:	N. Agadjanovoi
PHOTOGRAPHY:	Eduard Tisse
MUSIC:	Edmund Meisel
LEADING PLAYERS:	A. Antonov, Vladimir Barski, Grigori Alexandrov, Repnikova, Marusov, I. Bobrov
PRODUCTION COMPANY:	1st Studio Goskino
COUNTRY:	USSR
DATE:	1925

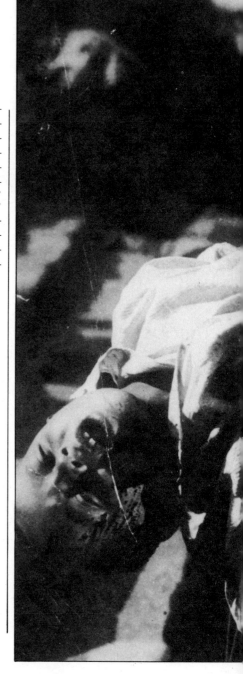

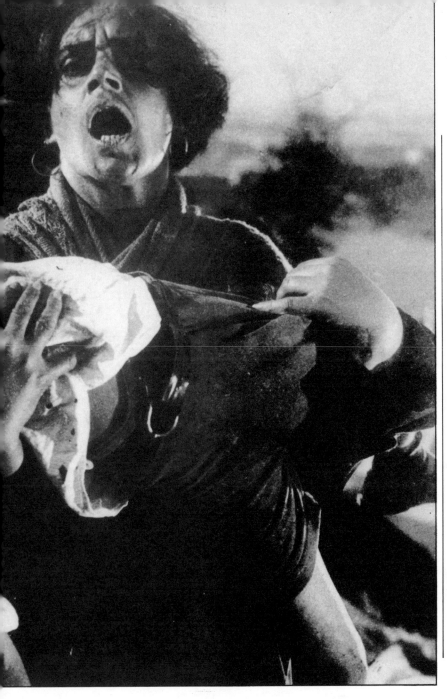

Eisenstein's most memorable sequences in the film – the maggots in the meat, the Odessa Steps, the hand-coloured red flag – had the intended incendiary effect. First banned in Berlin, a press campaign resulted in its eventual premiere, but German soldiers were warned in a special order not to see the film. Even so it was banned a second time, and the powerful baby-carriage scene had to be cut before it was again allowed to be shown.

When Brian De Palma was filming *The Untouchables* in 1986 and needed a sequence of terror and suspense, he lifted the famous baby carriage scene from *Potemkin*, and placed it almost intact in his own movie.

8 ½

OTTO E MEZZO

Why 8½? Because, for this most autobiographical of Fellini's films (a description he alternately rejected and acknowledged), which is not only about filmmaking, but is in fact about the making of itself, Fellini settled on the idea that he had already made seven films and a half, the half being a short episode from Boccaccio.

It is true [Fellini admitted] that inevitably all the episodes in 8½ refer to my life, but some of them gradually became distorted, while others took shape during the shooting. The result was the story of a director who must begin a film but cannot remember the plot and continues to oscillate between two planes: reality and imagination.

Those elements become confused, the director's ideas disintegrate, and his own life begins to lose any sense of meaning while all around him his wife, his mistress, his producer and everyone else within earshot demand decisions from him.

Casting itself took on Felliniesque overtones. Mastroianni was to play the 'Fellini' role of course, but Fellini actually put an ad in the paper for the role of Carla, the mistress. Sandra Milo was eventually chosen, and she put on twenty pounds for the part, some of which may have been attributable to the baby she was carrying and to which she gave birth at the time of the film's premiere. He also cast Caterina Boratto, an ageing actress from the 'white telephone' era; Guido Alberti, an industrialist who made Strega liqueur and who founded the Strega Prize for writing; and an 86-year-old tax department employee named Tito Masini who was discovered by chance leaving a library. Jean Rougeul played the critic Carini who was based on the actual Luigi Chiarini, one-time director of the Venice Film Festival.

Fellini was, as usual, secretive about the film's story. Even Mastroianni was not allowed to know exactly what was coming up next. Because Fellini had a spaceship constructed, to be used as a symbolic event in the film, it was rumoured that he was making a science-fiction movie. But Fellini explained his reticence in an interview:

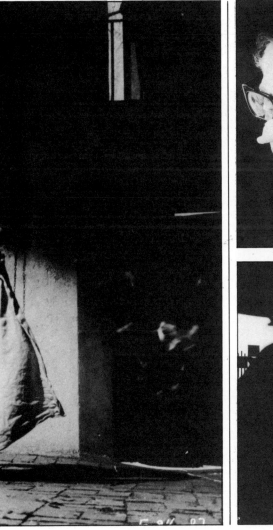

When I said that I didn't know what the plot was, journalists thought I was telling them one of my habitual lies. Instead, for me, it was the truth. I was looking for the Juno-like woman, I was busy, I appeared to have it all worked out in my head, but it was not like that. For three months I continued working on the basis of a complete production, in the hope that meanwhile my ideas would sort themselves out. Fifty times I nearly gave up.

But he did not give up, of course. Instead he threw in masses of autobiographical detail and the film, unlike the earlier *La Dolce Vita*, became a personal history of the man, Federico Fellini, and his art, film making. '8½ is a film of liberation – nothing more,' Fellini claimed. 'Unfortunately I know that intellectuals will go and dig up James Joyce (whom I have never read) and everything will run the risk of becoming confused. But I still maintain that it is a positive work, more positive than *La Dolce Vita*, and that it has not negative characters.'

8½, made in black and white because 'dreams are never in colour'(?!), won not only the major prize at the Moscow Film Festival, but also the Oscar for Best Foreign Film – the third such Oscar Fellini had won, and the one he claimed in person. It also obtained all the Italian Oscars given in secret by the Italian critics.

DIRECTOR:	Federico Fellini
SCREENPLAY:	Fellini, Ennio Flajano, Tullio Pinelli, Brunello Rondi
PHOTOGRAPHY:	Gianni Di Venanzo
MUSIC:	Nino Rota
LEADING PLAYERS:	Marcello Mastroianni, Claudia Cardinale, Anouk Aimee, Sandra Milo, Rosella Falk, Barbara Steele, Guido Alberti, Madeleine Lebeau
PRODUCTION COMPANY:	Cineriz
COUNTRY:	Italy
DATE:	1963

5 SINGIN' IN THE RAIN

'There are no auteurs in musical pictures,' Gene Kelly said when asked about his collaboration with Stanley Donen in *Singin' in the Rain*. 'It's impossible.' And if ever there was a movie to prove his point, this was it. Choreography by Kelly, directed by Kelly and Donen, screenplay by Comden and Green, produced by Arthur Freed, art direction by Cedric Gibbons, music and lyrics by Arthur Freed and Nacio Herb Brown, Comden and Green, and others, all of it was brought whimsically to life by Kelly, Debbie Reynolds, Donald O'Connor, and Jean Hagen. Take away any of these essential elements and *Singin' in the Rain* becomes less than the sum of its parts.

It was Freed's idea. He knew only that it would be based on the songs he and Nacio Brown had written more than twenty years before when he and his partner were brought to MGM to write the songs for the studio's first musical, *Broadway Melody*. Comden and Green came up with the idea of building the story around that shaky, unsure period when Talkies made their debut and the whole nature of the industry changed practically overnight.

They put together a silly, but engaging plot of a romantic silent star (Kelly) who falls in love with a chorus girl (Reynolds) and wants to make her his leading lady. But his current leading lady (Hagen), whose squawky shriek of a voice is failing miserably to make the transition to sound, isn't about to put up with that nonsense.

And so the film goes, playing off every showbiz cliché with a delightful combination of genuine homage and giddy irreverence.

'There had been real satires done [on Hollywood] of which we were blissfully unaware,' Kelly said. 'We felt it had to be a loving kind of satire. Everything that was kidded in it was the truth. All those things actually happened in Hollywood. We had many more incidents we didn't use.'

It was *Singin' in the Rain*, as much as anything, that substantiated in the public's mind the myth that many or most silent stars had tinny speaking voices. In fact, though many of them did fall prey to changes in the public taste which occurred at the same time, this had little to do with 'thin' voices.

DIRECTOR: Gene Kelly, Stanley Donen

SCREENPLAY: Adolph Green, Betty Comden

PHOTOGRAPHY: Harold Rossen, John Alton

MUSIC: Nacio Herb Brown, Arthur Freed, Adolph Green, Betty Comden

LEADING PLAYERS: Gene Kelly, Donald O'Connor, Debbie Reynolds, Jean Hagen, Cyd Charisse, Millard Mitchell, Rita Moreno, Douglas Fowley

PRODUCTION COMPANY: MGM

COUNTRY: USA

DATE: 1952

In fact, a silent star with the voice and personality which Jean Hagen brought to her unforgettable Lina Lamont would probably have sailed into the sound era like a breeze, on the arms of actors like James Cagney.

Kelly, who'd previously collaborated with Donen on *On the Town*, again insisted not only that he be allowed to work with Donen, but that he share direction credit with Donen as well. 'If I was in a scene, I didn't have to look at the camera or glance at the other actors. At the end I would just look at Stanley, and he'd say okay. . . . We were one mind working toward an end.'

The result was not an immediate critical success. *Singin' in the Rain* garnered only two Oscar nominations, one for the musical score, and one for Jean Hagen. (Donald O'Connor did get a Golden Globe Best Actor Award for his hilarious 'Make 'Em Laugh' number.) William Goldman wrote, 'People thought ho-hum, another Metro musical, but this wasn't only a musical, it's one of the finest films about Hollywood.' An opinion usually shared by people who normally don't like musicals.

But if the critics were generally unimpressed, audiences showed no such reservations. It was the number one money-maker in April, and the number ten grosser of 1952. And it catapulted the previously serviceable dancer Cyd Charisse, who only appeared in one musical number as a long-legged Louise Brooks-like silent enchantress, to stardom.

Since then it has become a perennial favourite, even spawning a 1985 British stage musical lifted directly from the film version though lacking everything but the songs. The original, energetic, wildly inspired and superbly crafted version remains firmly intact on film, even if, like *Citizen Kane*, it does distort the past and some of the people in it, to appeal to a larger audience.

An ironic footnote to this story about a star whose career was wrecked by sound, and the little girl whose voice made her a star, was the fact that 19-year-old Debbie Reynolds' singing voice was dubbed by Betty Noyes, and Jean Hagen dubbed Debbie's lines for the scenes where Debbie was supposedly dubbing for Jean's character!

6 MODERN TIMES

In 1935, well after the end of the silent era, Chaplin undertook to produce a feature film which was, for all intents and purposes, not a 'Talkie'. *Modern Times* took nearly a year to film, from October 1934 through August 1935, making it Chaplin's shortest shoot since *A Woman of Paris*. But Chaplin felt he spent too much time on it. 'When I had worked a scene up to perfection, it seemed to fall from the tree. I shook the branches and sacrificed them separately, one by one, like my early two reelers.'

When the film previewed in February 1936, audiences were brought up short by the audacity (or perhaps the reactionism) of doing a silent film in the mid-Thirties, and it is only with the passing years that we have been able to see *Modern Times* as the comedy of social comment it was intended to be. A dialogue script was in fact prepared for each scene, but in the end only sound effects were used, with occasional bits of spoken words. The first articulate words spoken in any Chaplin film come across a video screen in the factory, and they're spoken by the factory owner: 'Speed up.' The final sequence in the café required twelve days of shooting and 250 extras, and it was the first and last time the Tramp ever spoke on screen.

Modern Times is full of references to earlier Chaplin films, including the roller-skating scene (from *The Rink*), the restaurant scene (from *The Gold Rush*), and Chaplin's use of Chester Conklin and other players from the silent days. The opening sequence in the factory is generally acknowledged to have been 'borrowed' from René Clair's *A Nous la Liberté*.

At the heart of the film, of course, are the character of the Tramp and Chaplin himself, whose mime had never been more extraordinarily refined. Jean Cocteau once met Chaplin on board ship and described their meeting thus:

I do not speak English; Chaplin does not speak French. Yet we talked without the slightest difficulty. What is happening? What is this language? It is the living language, the most living of all and springs from the will to communi-

DIRECTOR: Charles Chaplin

SCREENPLAY: Charles Chaplin

PHOTOGRAPHY: Rollie Totheroh, Ira Morgan

MUSIC: Charles Chaplin

LEADING PLAYERS: Charles Chaplin, Paulette Goddard, Henry Bergman, Chester Conklin, Stanley Sandford, Hank Mann, Louis Natheux, Allen Garcia

PRODUCTION COMPANY: Chaplin/United Artists

COUNTRY: USA

DATE: 1935

cate at all costs in the language of mime, the language of poets, the language of the heart. Chaplin detaches every work, stands it on the table as if it were on a plinth, walks back a step, turns it where it will catch the best light.

This, perhaps better than anything else, best explains Chaplin's continuing power to amaze and delight audiences with his work. At the end of *Modern Times*, the Tramp walks off into the sunset, his pockets empty but his heart full and, this time, with the girl alongside.

WILD STRAWBERRIES

SMULTRONSTÄLLET

The wild strawberries of the title are a Swedish symbol for the emergence of spring, the rebirth of life. And so the characters in the film are concerned with life, and death, and their never-ending cycle.

Wild Strawberries springs from Bergman's own life. He was driving north to Dalama when he had a sudden desire to see his grandmother's house again.

It was the autumn of 1956 that I made the trip. I began to write the manuscript in the spring, as I remember. Because one of my best friends is a doctor, I thought it practical to make the central character a doctor. Then I somehow thought that this old man should be an old, tired egoist who had cut himself off from everything around as I had done myself.

The film concerns Isak Borg (Victor Sjostrom, himself, along with Stiller and Bergman, one of the great Swedish directors), a 76-year-old man who sets out to visit the University of Lund to be fêted on the 50th anniversary of receiving his degree. But the specific references in the film go back to Bergman's own experiences, among them Isak's dream where he discovers himself in a coffin. 'It was an obsessing dream. That it was I myself who lay in the casket was something I invented, but the part about the hearse hitting a lamp-post and the coffin falling out and dumping its corpse, I had dreamt many times.' And in Isak's final dream, he describes an old yacht as 'an ancient relic from the days of my parents' childhood, a mad impulse of our grandfather, the "Admiral"'. Bergman's own Grandfather Akerbloom was called 'the Admiral' because of a yacht he had bought. Isak's son Evald (Gunnar Bjornstrand) is exactly the same age as Bergman at the time the film was made.

While Bergman's earlier film *Smiles of a Summer Night* has been compared to, and has as its source, the operas of Mozart, the musical metaphor for *Wild Strawberries* has always been a Bach fugue, a complex structure of point and counterpoint expressing in its dense cinematic language the themes of death-in-life, and the atrophy of the emotional and spiritual selves.

DIRECTOR: Ingmar Bergman

SCREENPLAY: Ingmar Bergman

PHOTOGRAPHY: Gunnar Fischer

MUSIC: Erik Nordgren

LEADING PLAYERS: Victor Sjostrom, Bibi Andersson, Ingrid Thulin, Gunnar Bjornstrand, Folke Sundquist, Björn Bjelvenstam

PRODUCTION COMPANY: Svensk Filmindustri

COUNTRY: Sweden

DATE: 1957

THE GOLD RUSH

Remembered and loved more than any of his other comedies, Chaplin's tale of the Klondike gold rush was started in January 1924. His inspiration had been the rather macabre story of the famous Donner party who, stranded in the Rockies, had been reduced to eating shoestring and finally each other. Shooting for more than a year and then editing for nine weeks, he completed it in May 1925.

The first draft of the screenplay was called 'The Lucky Strike'. His new leading lady was still to have been little Lita Grey, who had previously appeared in Chaplin's *The Kid*, but after her Mexican marriage to him and pregnancy with the first of their two sons, she had to be replaced with Georgia Hale, by which time the title of the film had also undergone a change.

Alaska, including a small-scale mountain range with snow-capped peaks had to be recreated in the studio, and took some 500 scenic craftsmen nine weeks: to simulate the artificial snow and ice 200 tons of plaster, 285 tons of salt and 100 barrels of flour were required while four cartloads of confetti took care of the blizzard scenes.

Chaplin's famous chicken transformation scene had to be done in the camera, with a scene fade while Chaplin changed into chicken costume; film in the camera then had to be wound back and faded into the new scene. The movie was full of similar great set pieces: the feast the starving man made of eating the boots; the fight against the bear; his first dance with the girl; his struggle against the gale, and the drama when the hut is suspended over a precipice, and the dance of the rolls. This sequence had been dreamt up and 'performed' before, magnificently, in *The Cook* (1918) by Chaplin's former but since 'forgotten' co-star and comedic peer, Roscoe 'Fatty' Arbuckle. At the Berlin premier of *Gold Rush*, this sequence was so wildly applauded that the manager had to go to the projection booth and get the scene shown again, with the orchestra picking up the reprise.

This was the film Chaplin often declared that he would like to be remembered for. 'What I have done in this picture is exactly what I wanted to do. I have no excuses, no alibis. I have done just as I liked.'

DIRECTOR:	Charles Chaplin
SCREENPLAY:	Charles Chaplin
PHOTOGRAPHY:	Rolland Totheroh, Jack Wilson
LEADING PLAYERS:	Charles Chaplin, Mack Swain, Georgia Hale, Tom Murray, Malcolm Waite, Henry Bergman, Betty Morrissey
PRODUCTION COMPANY:	Chaplin/United Artists
COUNTRY:	USA
DATE:	1925

This is the name of the ugliest city in North-west Africa which means simply 'White House', a romanticized reproduction of which was created on the Warner Brothers Burbank Studio lot for a film to be called *Everybody Comes to Rick's*. In a stroke of Hollywood serendipity, the name of the film about three little people whose problems don't amount to a hill of beans in this crazy world got changed to *Casablanca*, previewed just as the Allies liberated the real place, and was on general release when Roosevelt and Churchill selected it as the site for their next wartime summit.

Bogart and Bergman weren't the first choices to play Rick and Ilsa. (It was going to be Ronald Reagan and Ann Sheridan/Michele Morgan/Hedy Lamarr, with Dennis Morgan in the Henreid role.) None of the principal actors knew in whose arms they would find themselves at the story's end – and they played their parts accordingly. And by that end, they had completed their transition from stars to superstars. Bogart's persona was given the romantic touch that would make him a legend, and Bergman would become every man's dream wife and every woman's ideal.

Casablanca is a masterpiece of the Forties, a classic entertainment, a huge hit from the moment of its release in 1942 when the film, director, and screenplay all won Oscars. It's a philosophical treatise on moral responsibility versus emotional needs and compulsions, and a definitive 'star' vehicle.

It's full of some of filmdom's most quotable lines – 'I'm only a poor, corrupt official' and 'Was that cannon fire, or is my heart pounding?' – and most often misquoted. 'Play it Sam, play . . . "As Time Goes By",' Ilsa pleads. Rick later demands: 'You've played it for her, you can play it for me. Play it!' But in the process of this film's absorption in a generation's consciousness, the lines became, 'Play it again, Sam.' When myth became fact, and it was printed as such, it became the title for Woody Allen's play about a man obsessed with heroes like Rick and women like Ilsa.

Unlike most of the other films in this list, *Casablanca* is also a tribute to the usually unsung but highly accomplished studio directors of whom Michael Curtiz was one of the best. Yet there is some dispute about how

DIRECTOR: Michael Curtiz

SCREENPLAY: Julius J. Epstein, Philip G. Epstein, Howard Koch

PHOTOGRAPHY: Arthur Edeson

MUSIC: Max Steiner

LEADING PLAYERS: Humphrey Bogart, Ingrid Bergman, Paul Henreid, Claude Rains, Conrad Veidt, Sydney Greenstreet, Peter Lorre, Dooley Wilson

PRODUCTION COMPANY: Warner Bros.

COUNTRY: USA

DATE: 1942

much Curtiz was responsible for the style and feel of the finished film. In an interview with John Tuska John Wayne claimed that Howard Hawks 'had done all the preparation work on the film but at the last minute he left the film and Michael Curtiz took the project over'. Hawks agreed. 'Well, Wayne is right. I did most of the preparatory work on *Casablanca*.'

Whatever the truth of the case, *Casablanca* contains something for just about every memory. Postwar, post-*Casablanca*, post-Bogart generations identify with the attitudes of the eternal anti-hero as perfected by Bogart, the man who embodied Raymond Chandler's classic dictum: 'Down these mean streets a man must go who is not himself mean, who is neither tarnished nor afraid.' They wax nostalgic about two people who sacrificed their love for each other because it's the right thing to do. And because they know the lines by heart. Like the song they all ask for, it only improves . . . as time goes by.

It took Kurosawa two years to convince a Japanese studio to produce *Rashomon*. Originally presented to the Toho studio, it was turned down as too much of a risk. Later, executives at Daiei, where Kurosawa went next, complained that they didn't know what the story was about, and that it was too short. Kurosawa obligingly added a beginning and an end to the film, which he had in turn based on two stories of Akutagawa: *Rashomon* and *In The Grove*.

In reality Kurosawa used little from the title story, and made a significant addition to the second – the role of the commoner. Even after the film had been made, quickly and under-budget thanks to elaborate pre-production, the producers did not respond well to it. The head of Daiei walked out of the first screening, and later, when it was ranked fourth in Daiei's box office, a lecturer/commentator was hired to talk through the film, attempting to let the audience know what it was about.

Rashomon probably would have been shelved except that the Venice Film Festival asked for a Japanese entry and the studio, on the recommendation of an Italian who had seen it in Japan and against the studio's own better judgement, submitted it for consideration. *Rashomon* went on to receive First Prize, shocking the Japanese who, above all, had thought the film too esoteric to be understood by foreigners. *Rashomon*'s success opened Western eyes to the Japanese cinema and helped to thaw the relationship between the cultures that had been frozen by the memories of the war.

A highly impressionistic film, it deals with the question of truth: what we believe to be the truth depends on how we see it, who is seeing it, and who is telling it. One literally receives impressions from the camera through light and image and sound. Kurosawa's actors, too, were encouraged to work towards this style. While waiting for the set to be finished, Kurosawa and his actors watched a 16 mm jungle film with a shot of a lion.

I noticed it and told Toshiro Mifune [the bandit] that that was just what I wanted him to be. At the same time Mori [the samurai] had seen a jungle

DIRECTOR: Akira Kurosawa

SCREENPLAY: Shinobu Hashimoto, Akira Kurosawa

PHOTOGRAPHY: Kazuo Miyagawa

MUSIC: Fumio Hayasaka

LEADING PLAYERS: Toshiro Mifune, Masayuki Mori, Machiko Kyo, Takashi Shimura

PRODUCTION COMPANY: Daiei

COUNTRY: Japan

DATE: 1950

picture in which a black leopard was shown. We all went to see it. When the leopard came on Machiko Kyo [the wife] was so upset that she hid her face. I saw and recognized the gesture. It was just what I wanted for the young wife.

Kurosawa's work not only became a major influence on the new herd of American directors like Paul Schroder, Coppola, George Lucas and others, but many of his films were re-made with great success as American westerns. *Rashomon* became a play, *The Outrage*, and a film starring Paul Newman.

THE BICYCLE THIEF/LADRI DI BICICLETTE

A film of such simplicity and directness that nothing seems to stand between you and the experience itself. Vittorio De Sica achieved this breathless realism through exquisite casting choices and a desire to tell, as he said, a 'simple and human story'.

Yet, somewhat amazingly, there were seven screenwriters involved in its making – Zavattini was the only one credited but others who worked on it included Oreste, Biancoli, Suso Cecchi d'Amico, Adolfo Franci, Gherardo Gherardi, Gerardo Guerrieri, and De Sica himself. They freely changed much of the novel on which the film was based. In the original, for example, the protagonist sets out to look for his stolen bicycle on a second bike he kept for emergencies.

Vittorio De Sica, himself a consummate actor, used non-professionals, whom he discovered through an uncanny instinct for talent and dogged persistence. De Sica cast Lamberto Maggiorani, a factory worker, when Maggiorani brought his own son in to audition for the role of Bruno. Lianella Carell, a journalist, was cast as Maggiorani's wife when she came to see De Sica in order to do an interview on the film. Enzo Staiola, who was cast as Bruno, was found by De Sica as he stood watching the shooting of the film itself. From all of them he drew performances that are heart-rending but without self-pity.

It's not a literate film, or even conventionally dramatic. But its sense of life, captured in its exquisitely portrayed relationships, made Italian realism comprehensible to a mass audience. De Sica said, 'In Italy men often go out with their sons. Children converse with their father, become confidants, and very often become no longer children, but "little me". This I think is universal.'

On its release, *Bicycle Thieves* was attacked by De Sica's compatriots on all sides, by the right-wing press for its unsavoury view of postwar Italy, and by the left-wing press for portraying despair instead of revolution. But the world at large embraced the film, and it went on to win the Oscar for Best Foreign Film of 1949.

DIRECTOR: Vittorio De Sica

SCREENPLAY: Cesare Zavattini

PHOTOGRAPHY: Carlo Monuori

MUSIC: Alessandro Cicognini

LEADING PLAYERS: Lamberto Maggiorani, Enzo Staiola, Lianella Carell, Gino Saltamerenda, Vittorio Antonucci, Guilio Chiari

PRODUCTION COMPANY: PDS (Enic)

COUNTRY: Italy

DATE: 1948

After everyone else in Hollywood talked and nobody else made a silent film, Chaplin, in 1931, continued to make what were basically silent films. He had started work on the film in 1928 but his only concessions to the new medium were to add a music score plus a gag, when he swallows a whistle, develops a hiccup which disrupts a musical performance and attracts the dogs in the neighbourhood.

Director Robert Parrish, who had begun as a child actor, and played a newsboy in the film, recalled,

As Chaplin passed in front of our corner, Austin Jewell and I raised our peashooters. Chaplin said, 'No, wait!' And promptly stopped being the Tramp and the blind girl and became two newsboys blowing peashooters. He would blow a pea and then run over and pretend to be hit by it, and then back to blow another pea. He became a kind of dervish, playing all the parts, using all the props, seeing and cane-twirling as the Tramp, not seeing and grateful as the blind girl, pea shooting as the newsboys. Austin and I and Miss Cherill (who played the blind girl) watched as Charlie did his show. Finally he had it all worked out and reluctantly gave us back our parts. I felt he would rather have played all of them himself.

Chaplin, interviewed in 1968, said, 'I had to correct and act and write and produce the film, cut it . . . and I did it all, which very few in my day did you know. They didn't do it all you see. And that's why I was so exhausted.'

DIRECTOR:	Charles Chaplin
SCREENPLAY:	Charles Chaplin
PHOTOGRAPHY:	Rollie Totheroh, Gordon Pollock, Mark Marklatt
MUSIC:	Charles Chaplin
LEADING PLAYERS:	Charles Chaplin, Virginia Cherill, Florence Lee, Harry Myers, Allan Garcia, Hank Mann
PRODUCTION COMPANY:	United Artists
COUNTRY:	USA
DATE:	1931

LES ENFANTS DU PARADIS

CHILDREN OF PARADISE

Amasterpiece of courage and freedom that emerged from what was perhaps France's darkest hour – the German occupation during the Second World War. Its theme of oppression versus the freedom of the artist was so subtly written by Jacques Prévert that the entire project was done with the consent of the German censors, and yet, the clarity of its message is today impossible to miss. The idea for the story came out of a meeting Prévert, Carne and Barrault had in Cannes, in 1942, when Barrault, who wanted to work with them, suggested a story about the celebrated panto-mimist Debureau. Prévert said that it took him six months to write the screenplay in collaboration with Marcel Carné, Mayo (the costume designer), Barsaq and Trauner (set designers) and the composer Joseph Kosma.

It was being shot at the Victorine Studios in Nice even as the Allied troops landed in Southern Italy and the company was ordered to return to Paris. The delay of two months before shooting could resume at the Joinville studios added a further 9 million francs to an already amazing budget which now reached 60 million francs.

It was the first film to be shown in France after the Liberation. In size, scope and dramatic sweep, it is the French *Gone with the Wind*. According to an interview with Marcel Carné in 1944, they had up to 1,800 extras on the set for some of the scenes, and at a time when the Vichy Government would not allow any film longer than 2,750 metres without special dispensation, *Les Enfants* was 5,000 metres.

It is a sound film, and yet features a mime artist (Jean-Louis Barrault) as the main protagonist. Garance (Arletty), the woman who is the spirit of the Children and the heart of the film, is also a forerunner of the modern emancipated woman, the type who would have been in the vanguard of the Free French movement (and whose character would have been yet one more reason for the German censors to object to the project).

The title refers not to the actors, petty thieves, ladies of the boulevards and mountebanks who populate the story, but to the young people, the children who sit in the gallery of the theatre. They are the common folk, to

DIRECTOR: Marcel Carné

SCREENPLAY: Jacques Prévert

PHOTOGRAPHY: Roger Hubbard, Marc Fossard

MUSIC: Joseph Kosma, Maurice Thiriet

LEADING PLAYERS: Pierre Brasseur, Léon Larive, Arletty, Marcel Herrand, Fabien Loris, Pierre Renoir, Etienne Dacroux, Jean-Louis Barrault, Maria Casarès, Pierre Palau, Albert Remy, Jeanne Dussol, Gaston Modot, Jeanne Marken

PRODUCTION COMPANY: SN Pathé-Cinema

COUNTRY: France

DATE: 1945

whom the actors play, seeking fame and adoration. Set in the turbulent Paris of the 1830s, the entire production, designed by the brilliant Jewish art directors Trauner and Barsaq, working in Nazi-occupied France, superbly evokes the style of the period. Yet the film also creates an unreal, fantasy world into which the audience escapes.

Critics have pointed to its heightened poetic qualities to insist that it is theatrical in style. Carné himself called it 'A tribute to the theatre'. More often this rich work has been compared to the great novels of the nineteenth century in its structure and its length – nearly three hours. But, while this is always meant as praise for the film, Prévert wrote not for the word on the page but for the light on the screen.

In 1979, twenty years after the Nouvelle Vague's shake-up of the French film industry and its rejection of that cinema's past and of commercial directors like Marcel Carné, the French Film Academy voted it the Best French Film of all time.

14 SUNRISE

Murnau was one of many European directors wooed and won by Holly-wood in the 1920s. Impressed by his 1924 German success *The Last Laugh*, William Fox successfully seduced him into an appealing contract and Murnau arrived in 1926, with the Fox Studio at his disposal. *Sunrise* was his first effort in 1927, created in a honeymoon period that allowed Murnau to produce his own personal vision.

Murnau worked on this film, based on Hermann Sudermann's story *A Trip to Tilsit*, in the German Expressionist manner he knew so well. Characters are known simply as The Man, The Woman, and The Woman from the City. The sets were built in a forced perspective, making them appear larger and more spacious than they actually were. And Murnau used midgets in the backgrounds to emphasize the effect further. A restaurant is made to seem as large and intimidating as a football stadium. It is a moody film, employing lighting to a degree rarely if ever seen before on film.

'On the big scenes,' said Charles Rosher, one of the photographers, 'such as the fairground and the face, I think we used more lights than had ever been used before.' Pacing, too, became essential in the use of a roving camera that moved everywhere – sometimes taking the point of view of the actor, so that the audience could understand their 'expression'.

Murnau said, 'We have our thoughts and also our deeds. James Joyce, the novelist, demonstrates this very well in his works. He first picturizes the mind and then balances it with action.' The film became one of the last great examples of fluid, dynamic camerawork before sound was introduced. The Oscar winning first cameraman, Charles Rosher recalled:

For some scenes, such as the swamp sequence, the camera went in a complete circle. This created enormous lighting problems. We built a railway line in the roof, suspended a little platform from it which could be raised or lowered by motors. My friend and associate Karl Struss, operated the camera on this scene. It was a big undertaking, practically every shot was on the move.

The actors, though they were the typical Hollywood romantic stars, drew on the 'German school' of acting. George O'Brien's performance can be traced to Emil Jannings in *Variety*. Murnau gave him lead boots in an effort to lend him the 'gorilla-like' walk demanded by the role. Janet Gaynor, for her part, won Hollywood's first Oscar for Best Actress in conjunction with this film, *Seventh Heaven*, and *Street Angel*.

Sunrise was influential and not just with directors like Borzage with his *Street Angel* and *The River*, but even with such down-home men as John Ford, who made use of the village sets in *Sunrise* for his own *Four Sons*. By the time of Murnau's second film for Fox, however, the honeymoon had faded. After his third film, which the studio took away from him, recut, and issued as *City Girl*, Fox tore up his contract. When Murnau was killed in a 1931 car crash, barely a dozen mourners showed up at the funeral.

In 1939 Veit Harlan directed a German remake entitled *Die Reise Nach Tilsit*, which, unlike most remakes of great classics, wasn't so bad.

DIRECTOR: F. W. Murnau

SCREENPLAY: Carl Mayer

PHOTOGRAPHY: Charles Rosher, Karl Struss

LEADING PLAYERS: George O'Brien, Janet Gaynor, Margaret Livingston, Bodil Rosing, J. Farrell MacDonald

PRODUCTION COMPANY: Fox Film Corporation

COUNTRY: USA

DATE: 1927

15 MADAME DE...

THE EARRINGS OF MADAME DE.../DIAMOND EARRINGS

The film was adapted from a short novel by Louise de Vilmorin. It tells of a pair of earrings, given by Monsieur to his wife, which are sold by her to pay off a debt, are bought back by the husband who gives them to his mistress, who sells them, and are next bought by a diplomat who falls in love with Madame De and gives them to her. Her husband, seeing them, realizes his wife's infidelity, returns them to the diplomat and tells him the story. Deserted by her one true love, the desperate woman goes into a decline and dies. Out of this story of infidelity in high society Max Ophuls constructed a masterpiece. At the time of its release, critics like Lindsay Anderson and Karl Reisz criticized it for over-decoration and over-elaboration of style.

Shortly after the film's release Ophuls gave his thoughts on film.

The story of a film is a riddle. I find it difficult to write about, because if one defines something full of secrets its beauty may be destroyed. . . . The masters of our profession, René Clair or Jean Renoir, for example, Jacques Becker in his late work, or John Ford in many of his early films, in their best moments of 'in-sight' transcend both dramatic structure and dialogue, and create a new kind of tension which, I believe, has never existed before in any of the other forms of dramatic expression: the tension of pictorial atmosphere and of shifting images . . . . where would people like us get to if we couldn't get carried away? If my overstatement of the case has just one result – sparking off the desire to see – then it will not have been in vain. For the pleasure of seeing should be the moving force behind my film story. If this pleasure is pure and strong and inflexible and each time born anew, then it can lead to film history. The person who can really let this feeling grow within himself is a 'seer' and therefore a film poet.

DIRECTOR:	Max Ophuls
SCREENPLAY:	Marcel Achard, Max Ophuls, Annette Wademant
PHOTOGRAPHY:	Christian Matras
MUSIC:	Georges Van Parys, Oscar Straus
LEADING PLAYERS:	Danielle Darrieux, Charles Boyer, Vittorio De Sica, Jean Debucourt, Lia de Lea, Mireille Perrey
PRODUCTION COMPANY:	Franco-London/Indus-Rizzoli
COUNTRY:	France/Italy
DATE:	1953

Jean Renoir's masterpiece on the themes of war, pacifism, and the creation of a new world order, *La Grande Illusion* is based on a true anecdote of a soldier who escaped numerous times from German POW camps during the First World War. Charles Spaak's script was turned down by numerous producers until Jean Gabin, the most popular French star of his generation, who would play the role of Marechal, joined the project.

When Eric von Stroheim became interested in the role of Rauffenstein, the German POW Commandant, that part was increased from a small five-minute appearance to become a major, dominating feature of the film. Von Stroheim, in his white gloves and neck brace – an idea he thought of himself to show that Rauffenstein had been invalided out of active service, has become the most familiar image of the film, symbolizing the old aristocrat order of Europe as it crumbles before the onslaught of the machine gun and the technology of modern warfare. *Illusion* allowed audiences to see that 'The Man You Love To Hate' also had a human face.

Four weeks were spent shooting exteriors in Alsace at the military barracks at Colmar, constructed by Wilhelm II. With this film, as with the later *La Règle du Jeu*, Renoir exploited the opportunities of chance and improvisation wherever possible, including casting, storyline, and characterization. All the characters have French as a common language, but they all speak their own language among themselves, with subtitles. Boieldieu, the aristocratic French hero, speaks English with Rauffenstein.

The film won the Special Jury Prize at the 1937 Venice Film Festival, but was banned in Italy until after the war. The Nazis were divided in their opinion. Goering, for one, liked it. But Goebbels described it as Cinematographic Enemy No. 1 and saw to it that it was banned. 'Von Stroheim's impersonation of a German officer is a caricature,' he protested at Venice. 'There are no German officers like that.' Franklin Delano Roosevelt said of it, simply that 'All Democrats should see this film.' Even so, the original version, in which a German woman and a French soldier live together and share a bed, was not shown even to Democrats, until 1958. And in America, the subtitles never included the word 'Jew', an omission about which Renoir protested upon seeing it translated for the first time.

The film has always enjoyed enormous popularity among audiences and critics alike. Basil Wright wrote that 'in criticising *La Grande Illusion*, it is necessary to stress the fact that it can only be judged by the very highest standards. Its values . . . are unquestionably in the first rank.'

Renoir said, 'I made *La Grande Illusion* because I am a pacifist.'

DIRECTOR: Jean Renoir

SCREENPLAY: Jean Renoir, Charles Spaak

PHOTOGRAPHY: Christian Matras

MUSIC: Joseph Kosma

LEADING PLAYERS: Jean Gabin, Pierre Fresnay, Erich von Stroheim, Dalio, Julien Carette, Gaston Modot, Jean Dasté, Dita Parlo, Péclet

PRODUCTION COMPANY: RAC

COUNTRY: France

DATE: 1937

17 *THE SEARCHERS*

John Ford, back again in Monument Valley where he first went for *Stagecoach* (1939), shot this 'tragedy of a loner' in 1955 in 55 days. It became a cult film for directors of the next generation – Scorsese, Spielberg and Lucas; Paul Schrader even re-worked the story into a modern tale of a man searching among the porno houses for his 'lost' daughter in *Hardcore*.

John Wayne was, as usual, at the heart of the film, and perhaps more so here than ever before. Ethan Edwards (Wayne) returns home from the Civil War three years after it is over, and the entire film deals with him: his search, his struggle. This was unusual for Ford, who normally gravitated towards groups of characters, and it was not typical of Wayne either, who was playing a figure more human, and less perfect, than usual.

The studio was well aware of Wayne's drawing power with an audience and pushed his dominant role in the film in their advertising despite the abuse he was getting from the critics. Ford seemed to understand and appreciate Wayne more than most other directors or Wayne's critics, apparently unconcerned that many saw the actor as wooden, incompetent, and incapable of an original characterization. Because the only kind of style actors like Wayne had at their command was that of their personality, there was always the danger they might petrify. But with some actors, and Wayne was one of them, petrification made for greatness. He had become like a statue of himself, like an auteur with a very consistent handwriting all his own.

Although the film has unmistakable racist overtones, Ford the director got along famously with the Navajo Indian extras. He paid them at regular union rates, studied their language, and was adopted into their tribe. That sort of behaviour contrasts sharply with the film itself, in which Old Mose, played by Hand Worden, prays before an Indian massacre: 'Oh Lord, for what we are about to receive, we thank you.'

The search for the abducted girl becomes, before the splendid Technicolor/Vistavision backgrounds, a quest for the 'inner man' as well. As the title song goes, 'A man will search his heart and soul, go searchin' way out there.' For himself, who chose not to explain the 'missing' three years between the end of the Civil War and Ethan's arrival home at the beginning of the film, said 'He's the man who . . . probably went over into Mexico, became a bandit, probably fought for Juarez or Maximilian – probably Maximilian because of the medal. He was just a plain loner, could never really be part of the family.'

Though unappreciated by the critics, *The Searchers* grossed $4.9 million in 1956, and was one of the most commercially successful films of its time.

DIRECTOR:	John Ford
SCREENPLAY:	Frank S. Nugent
PHOTOGRAPHY:	Winston C. Hoch
MUSIC:	Max Steiner
LEADING PLAYERS:	John Wayne, Jeffrey Hunter, Vera Miles, Ward Bond, Natalie Wood, John Qualen, Olive Carey, Henry Brandon, Ken Curtis, Harry Carey Jr, Hank Worden
PRODUCTION COMPANY:	Warner Bros.
COUNTRY:	USA
DATE:	1956

I have just seen your Space Odyssey. *My wife and I drove fifty miles to see it. During the return trip we tried to discuss calmly what we had seen, but we invariably ended up screaming at each other. Had we lived another fifty miles from the theatre we might possibly have worked something out by the time we got home – some sort of conclusion that we could have lived with.* Space Odyssey *cost me $5.00. I think, for my $5.00, I am entitled to some answers.*

So wrote Ansel H. Smith of Louisiana to Stanley Kubrick in 1969. As far as anyone knows, neither he, nor anyone else for that matter, has ever got an answer.

2001, which premiered in March 1968, just eight months before Apollo 8 was launched for the first moon trip, began production in December 1965. It was based on two works by Arthur C. Clarke, *The Sentinel* (only 11 pages long) and the novel *Childhood's End*. The narrative traces prehistoric man's discovery of weaponry (with the help of a mysterious black monolith sent by aliens from outer space), to a futuristic space voyage, the goal of which is to discover the origins of another monolith that has been discovered on the moon. In the course of the voyage, the ship's computer attempts to seize control, kills three of the astronauts on board, and is eventually 'killed' by the remaining one.

Kubrick controlled the production by shooting even the most exotic scenes like the African 'Dawn of Man' sequence in a studio. John Alcott, in charge of Additional Photography on the film, recalls that Kubrick wanted

a very weak light, like that of dawn, and it would have taken months to shoot each shot in Africa itself . . . Stanley constructed a 10″ × 8″ projector to project the background photographs on a screen . . . The transparencies were made up exclusively of photographs taken in Africa on Stanley's precise instructions. But the studio set was so large in the foreground that one really had the impresssion of being there.

Critics are still arguing over whether *2001* is a great, if confusing film, or if it is simply, as the Australian critic Clive James believes, 'trite'. *Variety*, in 1968, claimed it actually belonged 'to the technically slick group dominated by George Pal and the Japanese'.

As the above letter might suggest, audiences were often confused by the film's narrative and symbolism, but it didn't prevent them from making it a great, unexpected commercial success. Even with a running time of 141 minutes (Kubrick himself cut 20 minutes after the previews), people flocked to see *2001*, and their enthusiasm launched such relatively obscure classical works from its soundtrack as *Also Sprach Zarathustra* into the world of popular music.

DIRECTOR: Stanley Kubrick
SCREENPLAY: Stanley Kubrick, Arthur C. Clarke
PHOTOGRAPHY: Geoffrey Unsworth, John Alcott
MUSIC: Richard Strauss, Johann Strauss, Aram Khachaturian, György Ligeti
LEADING PLAYERS: Keir Dullea, Gary Lockwood, William Sylvester, Daniel Richter, Douglas Rain, Leonard Rossiter, Margaret Tyzack, Robert Beatty
PRODUCTION COMPANY: MGM
COUNTRY: GB
DATE: 1968

19 *SOME LIKE IT HOT*

Filmed in black and white, against the trend for major American films in the 50s, because Billy Wilder felt that two leading men disguised as women would become too much of 'a flaming faggot picture' in colour, the story (as often with the Austrian-born Wilder who had started his career as a screenwriter at UFA) had its origins in a 1932 UFA musical written by Robert Thoeren, with a Depression setting and the usual obsession with cross-dressing characteristic of German comedies. *Some Like It Hot* brings together themes that crop up in many of Wilder's films: farce, masquerade, impersonation, from Ginger Rogers posing as a twelve-year-old in *The Major and the Minor* to Jack Lemmon in *Irma la Douce*.

It was the first film co-authored by Wilder with I. A. L. Diamond who had written most of Monroe's dialogue in *Love Happy*, *Monkey Business* and *Love Nest*. And *Some Like It Hot*'s final, famous line, 'Well, nobody's perfect,' said by a philosophical Joe E. Brown when he discovers that his reluctant girlfriend is, in fact, a man, was written by Diamond.

Wilder had a strong cast and was so confident of the success of his film that he got Jack Lemmon (the role was originally meant for Frank Sinatra) to shake a pair of maracas between his lines, to allow the audience time to recover from their laughter at the previous line. And Tony Curtis, best known until then for his haircut, contributed a notable parody of Cary Grant for his impersonation of a millionaire yachtsman.

The film had a production cost of $2,800,000, though Monroe's already legendary problems meant that the film took six weeks longer to shoot than planned, and made it go half a million dollars over the budget. Her frustrated co-star's (Tony Curtis) widely circulated comment that kissing Monroe was 'like kissing Hitler' was reported back to her. Sharp as a diamond in her own right, she dismissed his petty remark as jealousy because 'I look better in a dress than he does.' Despite her lateness and apparent inability to learn her lines, even when written down and pasted on the set, on film she was in top form, and accounted to a large degree for the film's critical and commercial success and its enduring appeal.

DIRECTOR: Billy Wilder

SCREENPLAY: Billy Wilder, I. A. L. Diamond

PHOTOGRAPHY: Charles B. Lang Jr

MUSIC: Adolph Deutsch

LEADING PLAYERS: Marilyn Monroe, Tony Curtis, Jack Lemmon, George Raft, Pat O'Brien, Joe E. Brown

PRODUCTION COMPANY: Ashton/Mirisch

COUNTRY: USA

DATE: 1959

The films with which Eisenstein established himself and his credentials as a serious artist, the silent, Socialist-conscious masterpieces like *Potemkin* and *October*, proclaimed the artist's art as a service for society. *Ivan*, his last work for the screen, is a testament to the 'nature' of the artist. With *Ivan* he was serving the cause and *himself*, the part of him that he had denied when, after returning to Russia from his aborted visit to Hollywood, he criticized von Sternberg's *The Scarlet Empress* for its wasteful excesses. Now he not only emulated but sought to outshine that work, in style and virtuosity. For von Sternberg, Russia was Catherine the Great. For Eisenstein, it was Ivan the Terrible.

The Russian censors were not concerned with Eisenstein's 'nature', only with his nonconformist interpretation of the Muscovite Czar under whose tyrannical reign, the ground rules were laid that would lead Mother Russia to nationhood.

A historical fresco of sixteenth-century Russia, this film shows the fight waged by Czar Ivan against the boyars and the Church as well as his inner struggles stemming from the variance between duty and conscience.

The film was originally planned as a tetrology. The first part, completed in 1944, was given its first showing at the beginning of 1945. The film, Eisenstein, the actors Nikolai Cherkassov (Ivan) and Serafina Birman (Grand Duchess . . .), the cameramen Tisse and Moskvine, and composer Prokofiev, all received the Stalin Prize. By the time Sergei submitted the second part to the Artistic Council of the Ministry of Cinematography, they reported that '*Ivan* displayed ignorance of historic facts by showing Ivan the Terrible's progressive army of oprichniks as a band of degenerates in the style of the American Ku Klux Klan; and Ivan, a man of great will power and strong character, as a weak and feeble being, a sort of Hamlet.' The second part, not shown until 1958, long after Eisenstein's death, includes the only sequence he ever shot in colour.

The script was written in blank verse, in a stylized Old Russian, and the dialogue, given an almost operatic delivery, resembles incantations; it has

DIRECTOR:	Sergei Eisenstein
SCREENPLAY:	Sergei Eisenstein
PHOTOGRAPHY:	Eduard Tisse, Andrei Moskvin
MUSIC:	Sergei Prokofiev
LEADING PLAYERS:	Nikolai Cherkassov, Ludmila Tselikovskaya, Serafina Birman, Pavel Kadochnikov, Mikhail Zharov, Amvrosi Buchma
PRODUCTION COMPANY:	Central Cinema Studio, AlmaAta
COUNTRY:	USSR
DATE:	1941–5

a rhythm and serves like a chorus to the music of Prokofiev, which acts as a counterpoint.

The photography of Moskvine (interiors), Tisse (exteriors) contributed greatly to the texture of the film. For his final shot, an image with which to conclude the first part and bridge to the next, Eisenstein borrowed the sequence from Mauritz Stiller's *Sir Arne's Treasure*, as Ivan, framed in the window of his retreat, looks down on the snaking procession of the citizens of Moscow, lined up in the snow for as far as the eye can see.

Eisenstein had embarked upon a third part but he died leaving only ten minutes of edited footage.

JULES ET JIM

François Truffaut once said, 'I make films I would like to have seen when I was a young man.' *Jules et Jim*, his third feature, must certainly fall into this category. It is a sadly romantic tale of two men, Jules and Jim, in love with the same woman, Catherine, the sort of story that was the basis of countless sophisticated American comedy films of the Thirties, like Noël Coward's *Design for Living*, and Lubitsch's *Angel*, and almost every Claudette Colbert comedy in between. 'There are two themes,' Truffaut said, 'that of the friendship between the two men, which tries to remain alive, and that of the impossibility of living *à trois*. The idea of the film is that the couple is not really satisfactory but there is no alternative.'

Jules et Jim is one of the finer examples of the French Nouvelle Vague – a film of emotional value executed with technical panache. Scenes are overlapped, fast cutting is employed, the continuity is played with. Catherine, played by never-more-expressive Jeanne Moreau, makes her first appearance before a camera that zooms in on her face from all angles, captures it for a moment, then releases it in a series of freeze-frame close-ups. The romantic yet spiky music composed by Georges Delarue underscores that deliberate tension between technique and emotion.

Truffaut based his movie on a novel by Henri-Pierre Roche. Truffaut kept nearly all the elements of the novel, though he rearranged them freely – most notably in the character of Catherine, who became a composite of several women in the book. The story is told almost like a fairy tale, with an ironic, poetic narrative which accompanies the film.

Spinning and swirling images dominate the film: the spinning wheels of their bicycles, which refers no doubt to Truffaut's earlier short *Les Mistons* with Bernadette Lafont on her bike; the camera circling triumphantly around the statues on the Greek isle; and Catherine's song itself, 'Le Tourbillon', seems to sum up the sweeping style of the piece.

Despite its potentially scandalous subject matter and essential pessimism, *Jules et Jim* presented the world with a vision of great freshness, on which a 1980 remake by Paul Mazursky, *Willi and Phil*, did not improve.

DIRECTOR: François Truffaut

SCREENPLAY: François Truffaut, Jean Gruault

PHOTOGRAPHY: Raoul Coutard

MUSIC: Georges Delarue

LEADING PLAYERS: Jeanne Moreau, Oskar Werner, Henri Serre, Marie Dubois, Vanna Urbino, Sabine Haudepin, Boris Bassiak, Kate Noelle, Anny Nielsen

PRODUCTION COMPANY: Les Films du Carrosse/ SEDIF

COUNTRY: France

DATE: 1961

A film of John Ford firsts. His first film shot in Monument Valley to which he would return again and again; his first sound Western; his first collaboration with John Wayne since the silent days; the first to feature the 7th Cavalry riding to the rescue. Most significantly, though, *Stagecoach* is considered by general acclaim to be the first modern Western. There are so many elements of the film that have been imitated, both slavishly and respectfully, that its most original parts have become cliché. And not just in Westerns. Orson Welles claimed to have seen *Stagecoach* forty times before he directed *Citizen Kane*.

Dudley Nichols – a Ford favourite – wrote a screenplay, which many consider to be the peak of his uneven career, based on a *Colliers* magazine story by Ernest Haycox (which in turn was derived from de Maupassant's *Boule de Suif*). It assembles a motley group of characters, stereotypes some might say, and sets them off on their journey across the wilderness armed to the teeth with every possible cliché (or that which was to become a cliché). There is the drunken physician, the professional gambler, the prostitute, the faithful wife, the thieving bank manager, the meak little whisky sales-man, the sheriff, and, of course, his prisoner – the Ringo Kid, played by John Wayne. Andy Devine drives the coach.

Stagecoach contains many favourite touches, some of them carefully con-structed, others happenstance. Among the former are the music, the Oscar-winning adaptations of seventeen American folk tunes, and the authentic costumes.

Not merely a film of physical excitement, *Stagecoach* also possesses great charm as well, perhaps attributable today to its comfortable predictability. Ford clearly was not aiming for subtlety either in his story or his character-ization. His hand-picked cast (Walter Wanger had wanted Ford to use Gary Cooper and Marlene Dietrich) acted out the simple, straightforward nar-rative with a kind of no-holds barred directness. 'Raise your eyebrows and wrinkle your forehead,' Ford instructed Wayne during a scene with Claire Trevor. After ten years on the screen, it was the beginning of his career as an

DIRECTOR:	John Ford
SCREENPLAY:	Dudley Nichols
PHOTOGRAPHY:	Bert Glennon
LEADING PLAYERS:	John Wayne, Claire Trevor, John Carradine, Thomas Mitchell, Andy Devine, Donald Meek, Louise Platt, Tim Holt, George Bancroft, Yakima Canott
PRODUCTION COMPANY:	Wanger/United Artists
COUNTRY:	USA
DATE:	1939

actor and would culminate, thirty years later, in *True Grit*, with an Oscar.

The film was a great success when it opened. Sol Siegel of Republic Pictures, said 'If it's a Western they want to make, let them come to Repub-lic to learn how to make it.' Wayne was under contract to Republic and, eventually, Ford directed him there in two of his best-known films, *Fort Apache* and *The Quiet Man*. *Stagecoach* has been remade several times since, both on the big screen and on TV. The only thing memorable about these was the title.

23 | *VERTIGO*

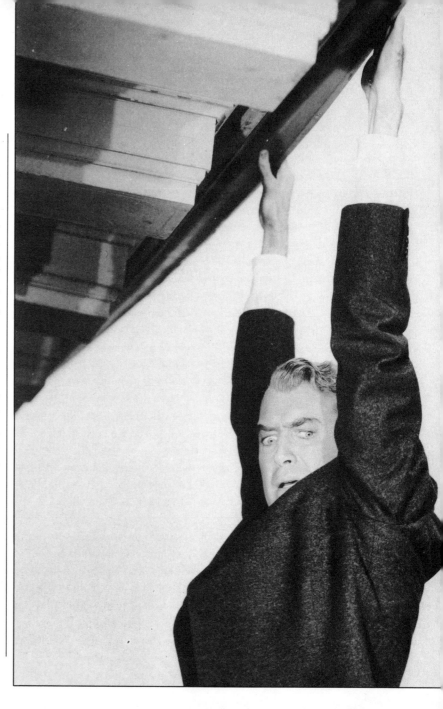

Pierre Boileau and Thomas Narcejac, whose previous novel *Les Diaboliques* had provided Clouzot with the plot for his classic thriller, also provided Hitchcock with the basis for *Vertigo* in their book *D'Entre les morts*. But where the novelists relied on the element of surprise, Hitchcock took his trademark route of suspense.

The film is divided into two parts. In the first, Scotty (Jimmy Stewart), a former detective who has left the police force because his affliction with vertigo caused the death of a fellow officer, is asked by an old friend to follow his wife Madeleine (Kim Novak), who he suspects is in danger of committing suicide. Scotty ends up falling in love with Madeleine, and the first part closes with Madeleine's death as she jumps from the tower of a Catholic mission. (There was no intended anti-Catholic symbolism here. The California Protestant churches didn't have towers. Or so, at any rate, the Catholic born and raised Hitchcock would have us believe.) So far, Hitchcock had followed the book.

But in the second half of the book, Scotty meets up with a girl, Judy, who seems to be Madeleine's double. He becomes obsessed by her, dressing her in Madeleine's clothes, trying to recreate Madeleine in her until finally, at the very end, both he and the reader discover that Judy and Madeleine are one and the same. Hitchcock, against the advice of those around him, fed to the audience the information that Judy and Madeleine are the same person early on in the second half.

I put myself in the place of a child [he said] whose mother is telling him a story. When there's a pause in the narration, the child always says, 'What comes next Mummy?' Well I felt that the second half of the novel was written as if nothing came next, whereas in my formula, the little boy knowing that Madeleine and Judy are the same person, would then ask, 'And [Jimmy] Stewart doesn't know it, does he? What will he do when he finds out? . . . . Our suspense will hinge round the question of how Stewart is going to react when he discovers that Judy and Madeleine are actually the same person.

DIRECTOR: Alfred Hitchcock

SCREENPLAY: Alec Coppel, Samuel Taylor

PHOTOGRAPHY: Robert Burke

MUSIC: Bernard Herrmann

LEADING PLAYERS: James Stewart, Kim Novak, Barbara Bel Geddes, Henry Jones, Tom Helmore, Raymond Bailey

PRODUCTION COMPANY: Paramount

COUNTRY: USA

DATE: 1958

The film is full of technical tricks and gadgets, and layers of visual meanings. In an effort to emphasize the double role/double image of the central character, Hitchcock told the art director Harry Bumstead with typical straightforwardness: 'Try to use a lot of mirrors.' Early in the first half, when Scotty follows Madeleine to the cemetery, Hitchcock gave her a dreamlike, mysterious quality by shooting through a fog filter. It gave the scene a green effect, like fog over the bright sunshine. And the famous shot down the stairway was done with a miniature shot on its side, using a tracking shot combined with a forward zoom. It alone cost $19,000 to shoot.

The film, along with *Marnie*, one of Hitchcock's most intensely personal, was a great success with audiences, though some have claimed they can barely believe Hitchcock intended it for commercial release. 'To put it plainly,' he once said in an interview with Truffaut, 'the man wants to go to bed with a woman who's dead; he is indulging in a form of necrophilia.'

THE SEVEN SAMURAI

SHICHININ NO SAMURAI

xplaining how the film which brought the Samurai to the West came about, Kurosawa once observed,

Japanese films all tend to be light, plain, simple but wholesome, just like green tea over cold rice, [a flavour so celebrated that Ozu even made a film with that title] but I think we ought to have both richer food and richer films. And so I thought I would make a film which was entertaining enough to eat, as it were.

Kurosawa had in fact wanted to make a *jidai-geki*, a period film, for quite a while. Even though half the films in Japan at the time were *jidai-geki*, he had never made one, and besides, they were generally compared to the American Westerns in their lack of substance. But, just as there were meaningful Westerns, so Kurosawa hoped to make a meaningful *jidai-geki*.

The original version ran 200 minutes but was cut to 160 minutes for its general release, and consists almost entirely of motion, either in the subject or in the camera. It won the Venice Festival Grand Prix.

Of his long collaboration with the film's star, Mifune, Kurosawa said:

Many actors unfortunately do not bother too much with creative process. They acquired several acting procedures and they then use them whether it is suitable or not. I often remember Mifune. When we worked together on Seven Samurai *we shot the scene in which he explains to the samurais the disgrace of the peasants and he cries. Mifune said to me, 'My hero is a peasant, and therefore he must cry like a peasant.' I was totally fascinated when he performed for me in front of the camera. In his acting performance there was always such remarkable sincerity and truth. When Mifune stood in front of the camera, I always watched the cameramen and lighting crew. I saw how they experienced everything with him and they cried too.*

It was especially pleasing that Kurosawa's film, having been made as a Japanese Western should, in turn, serve as the model for the remake *The Magnificent Seven*, a Hollywood Western that would revitalize that genre.

DIRECTOR: Akira Kurosawa

SCREENPLAY: Shinobu Hashimoto, Hideo Oguni, Akiro Kurosawa

PHOTOGRAPHY: Asakazu Nakai

MUSIC: Funio Hayasaka

LEADING PLAYERS: Takashi Shimura, Toshiro Mifune, Yoshio Inaba, Seiji Miyaguchi, Minoru Chiaki, Daisuke Kato, Ko Kimura, Kamatari Fujiwara, Keiko Tsushima

PRODUCTION COMPANY: Toho

COUNTRY: Japan

DATE: 1954

An elderly couple, living with their youngest daughter, decide to travel to Tokyo to see their older, married daughter and son. It proves to be a disappointment, they are sent to a resort, but feel unwell, and after a further night in Tokyo, the mother dies when they return home. Their children rush back but only the widow of their other son remains, caring for her father-in-law. But he advises her to re-marry and faces the future alone. The film is Ozu at his simplest and most masterful.

Mizoguchi said of him, 'I portray what should not be possible as if it should be possible, but Ozu portrays what should be possible as if it were possible, and that is much more difficult.'

The whole film is shot from the eye level of someone sitting down, Ozu's particular trademark. There is great simplicity in the shooting of the film, typical of Ozu, his style as exquisite as it was simple, with only a few establishing long shots, no tracking, panning, zooms, fades, or dissolves. Like the subjects of his films, the contemporary Japanese middle class family, Ozu was himself very conservative. He was one of the last Japanese to turn to sound, and his first colour film, *Samma No Aji (An Autumn Afternoon)*, was also the last film he made, yet, because of his low-level camera, his sets were constructed with ceilings long before the world applauded *Kane*'s innovations in that realm.

DIRECTOR:	Yasujiro Ozu
SCREENPLAY:	Kago Noda, Yasujiro Ozu
PHOTOGRAPHY:	Yushun Atsuta
MUSIC:	Takanori Saito
LEADING PLAYERS:	Chishu Ryu, Chiyeko Higashiyama, Setsuko Hara, So Yamamura, Haruko Sugimura, Kinoko Niyake, Kyoko Kagawa
PRODUCTION COMPANY:	Shochiku
COUNTRY:	Japan
DATE:	1953

ANDREI RUBLEV

onceived in 1961 but not seen in the West until 1971, the journey of the film from creation to release was nearly as tortuous as the life of the medieval Russian icon-painting monk it portrays. His second film, it was the first mature work by Andrei Tarkovsky; he was 32, the same age that Pushkin was when he wrote *Eugene Onegin*.

Tarkovsky's screenplay, suggested by the actor Vassily Livanov, who had been inspired by an exhibition of the artist's work in the official 1960 celebration of his sixth centenary, was co-written with Andrei Mikhalkov-Konchalovsky. It was begun late in 1961, after the year-long interruption of *Ivan's Childhood*, and completed by 1962, an era of liberalization in the Soviet Union. A production contract was signed in 1962, giving Tarkovsky full authority of his film; the literary scenario was accepted by the authorities the following year and the film was given the go-ahead in 1964. But by the time filming was completed a year later the Kruschchev era, and with it the openness that had marked cultural affairs during his chairmanship, was over. Suddenly, the Soviets discovered that they had a 'dangerous' film on their hands. Cuts were demanded for scenes showing nudity and violence. At first Tarkovsky refused. Eventually he did take out some 14 minutes and the now-standard 3 hour and 6 minute version was shown at Cannes in 1969 where it won the International Critics Prize. Meanwhile, in Russia it was not so much banned as 'held back' for release until 1971.

DIRECTOR: Andrei Tarkovsky

SCREENPLAY: Andrei Mikalkov-Konchalovsky

PHOTOGRAPHY: Vadim Yusov

MUSIC: Vyacheslav Ouchinnikov

LEADING PLAYERS: Anatoly Solonitsyn, Ivan Lapikov, Nikolai Grinko, Nikolai Sergey

PRODUCTION COMPANY: Mosfilm

COUNTRY: USSR

DATE: 1966

The cause célèbre of *Andrei Rublev* threatened to overshadow its artistic merit but Western audiences were not disappointed when it was widely screened in 1972. It is a work in two parts, epic in scale and length, biographical only in the loosest sense of the word. The real Rublev was a monk who painted, but Tarkovsky's aims were not historical. 'I do not understand historical films which have no relevance to the present. For me the most important thing is to use historical material to express Man's ideas and to create contemporary characters.' It is a gloomy picture of medieval Russia (though most films set around that era tend to be gloomy – *Richard III, The Seventh Seal*, gloom gloom gloom). An age of enormous upheaval and conflicts – pagan *vs* Christian, rich *vs* poor, old *vs* young, and of more significance in Russia at the time of the film's completion, it was also a story of social oppression and of the individual's moral obligation to stand against it.

It was shot in Scope – and partly, to great effect, in Sovcolor for the final meditation scenes where the brazier suddenly turns into colour, the charcoal transmuting into charred icons and the icons in turn become the paintings of Andrei Rublev.

FANNY AND ALEXANDER

FANNY OCH ALEXANDER

Possibly the most personal of any of his work, this was the first film Ingmar Bergman had made in Sweden since he completed *Face to Face* in 1975, before going into tax exile in Germany. He announced that with this family saga which was also a tribute and a celebration of his love of the theatre, he would be taking his farewell from theatrical films. The three-hour motion picture was first cut from 24 hours of film and then another cut was made for a five-hour television serial. He explained his decision to leave films:

Television is very different. It appears one evening and then – pssst – it's over! Gone! And I like that . . . . The thing I like best about a theatre performance is that it exists for a few evenings, perhaps a season. And then it's gone. . . . I hate all those festivals with my old pictures. I love the theatre because it is only that single moment.

The events are set in 1910 – and although Bergman moved the time of the story back seventeen years from his own childhood, it is as close to a direct autobiographical reminiscence as any that he has made. The ten-year-old Alexander is a self-portrait of the director. Bergman had two sisters, Margareta (Fanny) and an older sister, Amanda, who is included in the screenplay but not in the film version. Maj, the lame nursemaid, was based on Bergman's own nursemaid. The parents in the film were also based on his own. And most of the film's outdoor scenes were shot within a very small area on the west bank of the river Fyris, close to his grandmother's apartment.

. . . the making of Fanny and Alexander *was a fantastic time. A wonderful, funny, beautiful time – almost the best time of my life. Naturally it was difficult, and often I was tired to death. During a shooting period of seven months, anything can happen. Actors can become ill; we had an influenza epidemic that hit both Sven Nykvist and me. And one day a roof collapsed and almost killed us. So we lived constantly on the verge of catastrophe. But it was a good time, and I like my picture very much.*

It went on to win France's Cesar for the Best Foreign Film of 1983, and the American Academy Award for the same.

DIRECTOR:	Ingmar Bergman
SCREENPLAY:	Ingmar Bergman
PHOTOGRAPHY:	Sven Nykvist
MUSIC:	Daniel Bell
LEADING PLAYERS:	Gunn Walgren, Ewa Froeling, Jarl Kulle, Erland Josephson, Allan Edwall, Boerje Ahlstedt, Mona Malm, Gunnar Bjornstrand, Jan Malmsjoe
PRODUCTION COMPANY:	Cinematograph/SFI/SVTI/Gaumont/Personafilm/Tobis
COUNTRY:	Sweden
DATE:	1982

Two of the films that Jean Vigo made in his short life, *Zéro de Conduite* and *L'Atalante*, his only feature-length film, are both in the Top 100. It is a remarkable tribute to the achievement and lasting impact of a director who only made five films.

Vigo rewrote the script with Albert Riera from the original one by Jean Guinee about the life of a bargee on the river. He modelled the character of Père Jules (Michel Simon) to some extent on his own anarchic father.

Jean, a young bargee, marries Juliette, an even younger girl who is soon bored stiff by life on board. As France glides by she fantasizes about the glamorous life in the towns they pass, and relieves her boredom by visiting Père Jules, who shows her the treasures he keeps in his museumlike cabin: an elephant's tusk, a musical toy, a human hand preserved in a jar, and the nude tattoo dancing on his own back. Jean is viciously jealous and Juliette finally runs away when she sees her dream come true: a bewitching young man passing by on his bicycle. Jean pursues her and finds her. Reconciled, they return to the barge.

The film, surprisingly sensual for the period in conveying the feelings between the young people, moves between a sort of poetry and reality; although mainly shot on location (the creator of Maigret, Georges Simenon, advised on these), some studio work was also carried out but in deliberately constricted surroundings.

Shooting was affected by Vigo's bad health and his photographer, Boris Kaufman – Dziga-Vertov's brother and Vigo's link with the Russian cinema, who had by now photographed four of Vigo's films under Vigo's supervision – had to direct a few shots including the marvellous aerial image of the barge, with which the film ends.

But the sensuality of Vigo's style comes through loud and clear. His nuances and genius for portraying the secret rather than the public life of his characters went unappreciated on the film's release. It was shown at the 1934 Venice Film Festival but it attracted little interest on its Paris premiere and was soon taken off. Shortly after, Vigo died. Since then, the simplicity of *L'Atalante*'s story and the poetry of Vigo's vision, which never resorts to extravagant symbolism, have captured the imagination of succeeding generations.

DIRECTOR:	Jean Vigo
SCREENPLAY:	Jean Vigo, Albert Riera
PHOTOGRAPHY:	Boris Kaufman, Louis Berger
MUSIC:	Maurice Jaubert
LEADING PLAYERS:	Jean Dasté, Dita Parlo, Michel Simon, Gilles Mararitis, Louis Lefebvre, Maurice Gilles, Raya Diligent
PRODUCTION COMPANY:	J. L. Nounez-Gaumont
COUNTRY:	France
DATE:	1934

Viridiana follows most closely my personal traditions in film-making since I made L'Age d'Or thirty years ago. In all my work, these are the two films which I directed with the greatest feeling of freedom.

Viridiana *is very Spanish, and it must be understood that Viridiana was a little-known saint who lived in the period of St Francis of Assisi. The story is born of this situation – a young woman drugged by an old man, is at his mercy, whereas in other circumstances he could never be able to hold her in his arms.*

In reality Viridiana *is a picture of black humour, without doubt corrosive, but unplanned and spontaneous, in which I express certain erotic and religious obsessions of my childhood.*

. . . . I think that it has in it most of the themes which are closest to me and which are my most cherished interests.

I am against conventional morals, traditional phantasms, sentimentalism and all that moral uncleanliness that sentimentalism introduces into society . . . . Bourgeois morality is for me immoral and to be fought. The morality founded on our most unjust social institutions, like religion, patriotism, the family, culture: briefly, what are called 'the pillars of society'.

Thank God – I am still an atheist.

Before each shot Buñuel would wander about with a viewer, all by himself, for half-an-hour, lining up and planning the shot while the crew sat drinking. Then he'd go over and say, 'Right, this is what I want.' Then they'd go and get the shot, while he sat drinking.

DIRECTOR: Luis Buñuel

SCREENPLAY: Luis Buñuel, Julio Alejandro

PHOTOGRAPHY: Jose A. Aguayo

MUSIC: Gustavo Pittaluga

LEADING PLAYERS: Silvia Pinar, Fernando Rey, Francisco Rabal, Margarita Lozano

PRODUCTION COMPANY: Uninci Films 59

COUNTRY: Spain

DATE: 1961

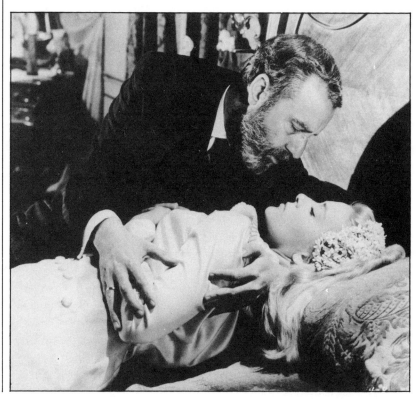

For anyone not English-born, *Kind Hearts and Coronets* more than any other single British film seems to be the film about this island race as they imagine it, much as Jean Gabin and films like *Le Jour Se Lève* seemed to sum up France and the French. It was written and directed by Robert Hamer and the title comes from a Tennyson couplet: 'Kind hearts are more than coronets/And simple faith than Norman blood.' The French, rather more delightfully, called it *Noblesse Oblige*. Producer Michael Balcon told his director, 'You are trying to sell the most unsaleable commodity to the British – irony. Good luck to you.'

Hamer, in an introduction to an extract from his script, wrote,

What were the possibilities which thus presented themselves? Firstly, that of making a film not noticeably similar to any previously made in the English language. Secondly, that of using the English language – which I love, in a more varied, and to me, more interesting way than I have previously had the chance of doing in a film. Thirdly, is that of making a picture which paid no regard whatever to established, although not practised moral conventions. This last was not my desire to shock, but from an impulse to escape the somewhat inflexible and unshaded characterisation which convention tends to enforce in scripts.

The ending was left ambiguous in the British version, leaving the public to decide whether the wicked (and charming) Louis (probably the finest role that Dennis Price played in the cinema) would get away with it, but in America it was necessary to show the manuscript of the confession actually in the hands of the authorities so that it was clear he would get punished.

The film of course marked the elevation of Alec Guinness to the front rank of British film stars. Originally offered three of the roles of the doomed D'Ascoynes, he suggested why not all seven, including the redoubtable Lady Agatha who met her demise through an arrow in her hot-air balloon, with the memorable valedictory from Louis, 'I shot an arrow in the air/She fell to earth in Berkeley Square.'

DIRECTOR: Robert Hamer

SCREENPLAY: Robert Hamer, John Dighton

PHOTOGRAPHY: Douglas Slocombe

MUSIC: Mozart

LEADING PLAYERS: Alec Guinness, Dennis Price, Joan Greenwood, Valerie Hobson, Audrey Fields, John Penrose, John Salew, Hugh Griffith, Arthur Lowe

PRODUCTION COMPANY: Ealing Studios

COUNTRY: GB

DATE: 1949

31   *THE THIRD MAN*

'I paid my last farewell to Harry a week ago, when his coffin was lowered into the frozen February ground, so that it was with incredulity that I saw him pass by, without a sign of recognition, among a host of strangers in the Strand.' With that irresistible teaser, Graham Greene hooked Alexander Korda on the idea of producing *The Third Man*.

Korda sent him to Vienna, a city literally devastated by war, to research a film concerning the four-power occupation of the city. Greene discovered a complex political and military arrangement there, with Vienna divided into American, Russian, French, and British zones, the four powers administering the Inner City for a month at a time on a rotating schedule, and patrolling the entire place day and night. After three months of poking around the ruined capital, Greene had lunch with a British intelligence officer who described the city's complex sewer system and, coincidentally, a penicillin racket then operating. These details, together with the other bits and pieces he had picked up, were all Greene needed: 'I had my film.'

Greene first wrote the screenplay as a story. 'One cannot make the first act of creation in script form,' he said, 'one must have the sense of more material than one needs to draw on.' He worked with Carol Reed on the actual screenplay. 'That is to say, I would do a section which I would hand to him while he was lying in bed and then we'd discuss it later.'

One of the many significant changes the script went through was the condensation of Tombs and Carterswere into the single character of Crabbin, played by Wilfrid Hyde White. Orson Welles' famous speech about cuckoo clocks in the ferris wheel was inspired mainly by Welles.

Their arrival in Vienna to begin location shooting was a great disappointment to Reed, who found that, in the intervening period between Greene's last visit there, many of the ruins had been cleared away and decent food was again being served in restaurants. Greene found himself saying over and over – 'But I assure you Vienna was like that – three months ago.' Still, they managed to find locations that were eerily real – bomb sites, misty cemeteries, wet night streets. (Robert Krasker, Director of Photography, was one of the first to punch up the atmosphere of night shots by spraying water on the streets.) The soon to become ubiquitous 'Harry Lime Theme' came about because of Reed's chance selection of a local café in which Anton Karas played a zither for tips.

The combination of happy coincidence and gritty, compelling story made *The Third Man* a critical success. In 1949, it won the Grand Prix for Best Feature Film at Cannes, and went on to inspire a popular and long-running radio series – using Orson Welles and the musical theme.

DIRECTOR:	Carol Reed
SCREENPLAY:	Graham Greene
PHOTOGRAPHY:	Robert Krasker
MUSIC:	Anton Karas
LEADING PLAYERS:	Joseph Cotten, Orson Welles, Alida Valli, Trevor Howard
PRODUCTION COMPANY:	London Films
COUNTRY:	GB
DATE:	1949

Ugetsu and *O-Haru* are Mizoguchi's two acknowledged masterpieces, of which *Ugetsu* is probably the most widely known and celebrated of his 33 films made over a career spanning 35 years until his death in 1956 of leukemia at the age of 58. Coming on the heels of *O-Haru*, *Ugetsu* again took the Silver Lion in Venice in 1953.

The film was based on the sixteenth-century legend of the same name (English title: *Tales of the Pale and Mysterious Moon After the Rain*), its author, Akenari Ueda, was considered the Japanese equivalent of Guy de Maupassant. It tells the story of two peasants who abandon family happiness for the illusion of fame, money and a magical woman. It was much admired by the French and is visually very sophisticated – misty scenes on lakes and rivers with men and lanterns on boats and spirits floating over the waters though the realistic scenes do lack something. According to Akira Kurosawa, 'In *Ugetsu*, when we get to the war scenes it just isn't war.'

DIRECTOR: Kenji Mizoguchi

SCREENPLAY: Matsutaro Kawaguchi, Giken Yoda

PHOTOGRAPHY: Kazuo Miyagawa

MUSIC: Fumio Hayasaka

LEADING PLAYERS: Machiko Kyo, Mitsuko Mito, Kinuyo Tanaka, Masayuki Mori, Sakae Ozawa

PRODUCTION COMPANY: Daiei

COUNTRY: Japan

DATE: 1953

33 *ZÉRO DE CONDUITE*

ZERO FOR CONDUCT

Only 45 minutes long, *Zéro de Conduite* is an autobiographical film, at least to some extent, as Vigo himself went through a certain amount of suffering at boarding school. The title refers to the mark the boys get when they don't come up to scratch, but the film is about more than the youthful rompings and misdeeds.

From the opening moments, in which the two young boys gradually change ordinary objects into wonderful effects and the only adult is declared 'dead', it is, in a sense, a magical, make-believe world where reality itself can be transformed. Later we discover that the Headmaster is a midget with a large top hat which he keeps under a jar in his office. And, in the film's most famous scene, the boys start a pillow fight in their dormitory in which the feathers from the pillows become a sort of magical snowstorm as the film gears down into slow motion.

In some ways the film is a primitive effort, with production supervised by Henri Storck, the Belgian documentarist, and photographed by Boris Kaufman, who contributed greatly to this and Vigo's other five films (in part because of Vigo's ongoing ill health). The finely appropriate music by Maurice Jaubert, which was re-scored, recorded in reverse, and then re-recorded backwards to restore it, achieves a dreamlike effect for the nightmare revolt.

Zéro de Conduite was banned by the French Board of Censorship in August 1933 and not released again until after the Second World War. Its impact on films of youthful rebellion can be seen over and over in the works of other directors, but possibly in no more notable instances than Truffaut's *Les 400 Coups* and Lindsay Anderson's *If . . . .*

DIRECTOR: Jean Vigo

SCREENPLAY: Jean Vigo

PHOTOGRAPHY: Boris Kaufman, Louis Berger

MUSIC: Maurice Jaubert

LEADING PLAYERS: Jean Daste, Robert Le Flon, Delphin, Du Verron, Blanchar, Larive, Louise de Gonzague-Frick, Raphael Diligent, Louis Lefebvre, Pruchon, G. de Bedarieux, Kelber, C. Goldstein

PRODUCTION COMPANY: Gaumont-Franco-Film-Aubert

COUNTRY: France

DATE: 1933

'If you were like him, with only half a year to live, what would you do?' The central question of Kurosawa's *Ikiru (Living)* is literally asked by the doctor of his assistant in the course of the film, but it is the film itself which answers.

Divided in half, *Ikiru*'s first hour is a long funeral scene (alternatively described as 'interminable' and 'an unbelievably bold piece of story-telling') intercut with flashbacks to the life of Watanabe, the petty official at the heart of the film. 'For a whole hour', writes the French critic André Bazin, 'we watch and listen to friends, relatives, and colleagues who have come to the funeral, as they talk about the dead man . . . these conversations are intercut with flashbacks which gradually reveal to us what the hero did before his death, and thereby his true personality.' Kurosawa's point was double edged: a meditation on death, and a film reflecting contemporary Japan.

And his methods were typically loose and exploratory:

I never write the script as though it were a closed or finished form. I start by visualizing just the first scene. There is a certain kind of character, with a certain kind of potential, and he is in a certain kind of position. Then if this character has it in him he begins to move by himself. And until he starts to move, it is very hard work. It may take months of thinking about. When he finally begins to move, then we all talk it over.

Nowhere in the film does the character of Watanabe 'begin to move' more significantly than in the coffee shop scene, where he has gone with a younger girl. Kurosawa sets up an array of contrasts with music, first the Pouppe Valsante, then the Parade of the Wooden Soldiers characters (the old and the youthful).

And then finally as Watanabe remembers the petition about the children's playground, and realizes he can *do* something, the young people at the coffee shop, celebrating a birthday, sing 'Happy Birthday to You' in a broken sort of English.

DIRECTOR:	Akira Kurosawa
SCREENPLAY:	Shinobu Hashimoto, Hideo Oguni
PHOTOGRAPHY:	Asakazu Nakai
MUSIC:	Fumio Hayasaka
LEADING PLAYERS:	Takashi Shimura, Nobuo Kaneko, Kyoko Seki, Makoto Kobori, Kumeko Urabe, Yoshie Minami, Miki Odagiri, Kamatari Fumiwara
PRODUCTION COMPANY:	Toho
COUNTRY:	Japan
DATE:	1952

APU TRILOGY

(1) PATHER PANCHALI (2) APARAJITO (THE UNVANQUISHED)
(3) APUR SANSAR (THE WORLD OF APU)

Satyajit Ray started his epic trilogy, the only one in the list (*Ivan the Terrible* was planned as a trilogy but only two parts of it were completed before Eisenstein's death), with a 16mm camera and an initial budget of £710. Ray, who had illustrated an abridgement of the famous novel, obtained the rights for a very small sum of money ($1300) due to his involvement with the work. The money was made up of a loan against his life insurance policy and money from his relatives. While the film was half finished and Ray was still looking for money, the footage was seen and encouraged by John Huston who was in India working on the idea of filming *The Man Who Would Be King* (which, years later, he eventually made). *Pather Panchali* was halted for eight months due to lack of money and after the West Bengal government purchased all rights to it in exchange for some Rs200,000 to finish the film, Ray ended up by receiving nothing!

Subir Bannerjee (Apu) was discovered by Ray's wife playing next door, after Ray had searched numerous schools for someone to play the role of the boy. There were only two professionals in the cast of *Pather*: Rebi Devi as the rich, nut-chewing neighbour, and Chunibala Devi, an 80-year-old former actress. Day scenes utilizing the village house were all shot in natural light, to the cynical amusement of the professionals who watched Subrata Mitra at work.

The film was only entered for Cannes, following a screening in London, at the instigation of James Quinn, then director of the BFI and a member of the Cannes Jury. It went on to win the Best Human Document, Cannes Film Festival 1956; and the David Selznick Golden Award, Berlin 1957.

Aparajito (*The Unvanquished*), which deals with the estrangement of Apu from his mother, was voted Best Film, Venice 1957.

In the second part, Mitra and Ray conceived the idea of using reflected, or bounced, light; it very effectively created a sense of daylight disguising the fact that they were filming on a reconstructed set of the original house.

In the final part, *Apur Sansar* (*The World of Apu*), Apu had become a father himself, of Kajal, a difficult son. It won the Sutherland Trophy Award, at the 1960 London Film Festival.

The trilogy, although not originally conceived as such, were shot in black and white and took Ray over eight years to complete. Ray and his films were – not merely in the storyline but in every sense – a challenge to traditional Indian concepts of movie-making in their lighting, dialogue and action. Their success abroad – the first Indian films to have a genuine critical success in the West – helped to open up the Indian cinema to the rest of the world. This was something which the long-established, hugely popular, native product had singularly failed to do.

Pather Panchali

DIRECTOR: Satyajit Ray

SCREENPLAY: Satyajit Ray

PHOTOGRAPHY: Subrata Mitra

MUSIC: Ravi Shankar

LEADING PLAYERS: Kanu Banerjee, Karuna Banerjee, Subir Banerjee, Uma Das Gupta

PRODUCTION COMPANY: West Bengal government

COUNTRY: India

DATE: 1952-55

Aparajito (The Unvanquished)

DIRECTOR: Satyajit Ray

SCREENPLAY: Satyajit Ray

PHOTOGRAPHY: Subrata Mitra

MUSIC: Ravi Shankar

LEADING PLAYERS: Pinaki Sen Gupta, Kanu Banerjee, Subodh Gangulyt

PRODUCTION COMPANY: Epic Films Private Ltd

COUNTRY: India

DATE: 1956

Apur Sansar

DIRECTOR: Satyajit Ray

SCREENPLAY: Satyajit Ray

PHOTOGRAPHY: Subrata Mitra

MUSIC: Ravi Shankar

LEADING PLAYERS: Soumitra Chatterji, Sharmila Tagore, Shapan Mukerji, S. Aloke Chakravarty

PRODUCTION COMPANY: Satyajit Ray prods.

COUNTRY: India

DATE: 1958

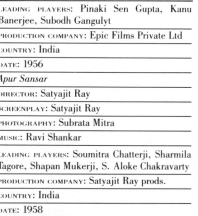

THE BAND WAGON

Writers Comden and Green, following their success of the previous year with *Singin' in the Rain*, based on the Freed and Brown song-catalogue, which had affectionately satirized the early days of Hollywood talkies, turned their attention to Broadway, using the songs of Freed's friends Schwartz and Dietz as their basis.

Producer Arthur Freed said,

I started out with the Howard Dietz and Schwartz music. Some of the songs were from the musical of the same name they wrote for Astaire and his sister Adele, but we scrapped that story, and used other songs they wrote as well. Dietz was then one of our vice-Presidents. (Jack) Buchanan was an accident in the picture. I had originally wanted Clifton Webb for the role of the egomaniac Broadway director, but he thought the character wasn't sarcastic enough and suggested I take Buchanan, who'd been a big musical comedy star in Britain. Cyd Charisse was probably Fred's best partner.

Director Vincente Minnelli said,

The Band Wagon, *being about the theatre, the ballet that would climax the story had to be a number you could do on a stage, and had to be something that was popular at that time, because the idea of the story was that the director (Jack Buchanan), who was very artistic and impractical, ruined the show. Astaire took it over, made it popular, jazzy, and that's what the people liked. As Mickey Spillane's novels were very popular at that time, I made it a satire on those private-eye novels. They're almost a satire in themselves. I made it in the spirit of Mickey Spillane, with beautiful girls, gangsters, killings, and private eyes.*

Unlike all the other songs in the film which had come from 1930s musicals the closing number and the film's most famous song, 'That's Entertainment', was written specially for the film. *The Band Wagon* is one of the favourite musicals of people who *like* musicals.

DIRECTOR: Vincente Minnelli
SCREENPLAY: Betty Comden, Adolph Green
PHOTOGRAPHY: Harry Jackson
MUSIC: Arthur Schwartz
LYRICS: Howard Dietz
LEADING PLAYERS: Fred Astaire, Cyd Charisse, Oscar Levant, Nanette Fabray, Jack Buchanan, James Mitchell
PRODUCTION COMPANY: MGM
COUNTRY: USA
DATE: 1953

It received more Academy Awards than any film to that date, a record it held until *Ben Hur*. Victor Fleming received the Oscar for Best Director though large proportions of the film were directed by George Cukor (who began the project), Sam Wood and others. Taking into account inflation, it remains the biggest moneymaker in the history of the American cinema. Some of the numerous books relating to it include:

Behlmer, Rudy (ed.), *Memo from David O. Selznick* (1972)

Chierichetti, David, *Hollywood Costume Design* (1976)

Edwards, Anne, *Vivien Leigh: A Biography* (1977)

Farr, Finis, *Margaret Mitchell of Atlanta* (1965)

Flamini, Roland, *Scarlet, Rhett and a Cast of Thousands* (1975)

Harwell, Richard (ed.), *Margaret Mitchell's G.W.T.W. Letters* (1976)

Haver, Ronald, *David O. Selznick's Hollywood* (1981)

Havilland, Olivia de, *Every Frenchman Has One* (1962)

Howard, Leslie Ruth, *A Quite Remarkable Father* (1959)

Lambert, Gavin, *G.W.T.W.* (1973)

Leab, Daniel J., *From Sambo to Superspade*

Noble, Peter, *The Negro in Films* (1952)

Pratt, William, *Scarlett Fever* (1977)

Russell Taylor, John, *Vivien Leigh* (19   )

Samuels, Charles, *The King: A Biography of Clark Gable* (1963)

Thomas, Bob, *Selznick*

Walker, Alexander, *The Life of Vivien Leigh* (1985)

It was the first time a major Academy Award was given to a black performer, when Hattie McDaniel won Best Supporting Actress for her role as the loyal Mammy, the maid and mainstay of Scarlett's family. Miss McDaniels, like the rest of the cast, had to learn the Southern accent for her role. It would be more than twenty years before another black performer (Sidney Poitier) won an Oscar.

Daniel J. Leab writes in *From Sambo to Superspade,*

DIRECTOR:	Victor Fleming
SCREENPLAY:	Sidney Howard
PHOTOGRAPHY:	Ernest Haller, Lee Grames (uncredited)
MUSIC:	Max Steiner
LEADING PLAYERS:	Clark Gable, Vivien Leigh, Leslie Howard, Olivia De Havilland, Thomas Mitchell, Hattie McDaniel
PRODUCTION COMPANY:	Selznick/MGM
COUNTRY:	USA
DATE:	1939

The most faithful of faithful souls is Scarlett O'Hara's ever scolding but ever loyal Mammy, who stays with her mistress through good times and bad, through Civil War and after . . . In most of the forty movies she appeared in before and after Gone with the Wind, *until her death in 1952, her roles were variations on the same part. She was obviously unhappy with this type-casting, [who isn't?] but she also recognized if she did not play the role on screen, she would end up playing it in real life.*

38   THE MALTESE FALCON

After a string of credits as a top screenwriter John Huston, as part of his new deal with Warner Bros to direct, was asked what he wanted to do. He mentioned Dashiell Hammett's *The Maltese Falcon*, 'The stuff that dreams are made of', a detective story filled with basically unpleasant or unscrupulous people. Even the hero, Sam Spade, sends the woman he may love to the gallows. It had already been filmed twice before (in 1931 and 1936, as *Satan Met a Lady*), and later, in 1975, as *The Black Bird*, a send-up) never very successfully. 'It would be a re-make of a story they owned and could be done for a very limited budget. I think the picture came to be made for under $300,000, which was much more than what $300,000 is today. Nevertheless it was a small budget for a Warner Bros picture.' Hammett's novel had been set in 1928–9 and Huston updated it to his own time.

Letting Hammett's own sparse style be his guide, Huston allowed the spare settings and minimal camera movement to serve as counterpoint to the intricate plot and its devious characters. Faithful to the book, he sought suspense not through monotonous car chases and the obligatory gunfights but rather, in the tradition of Hitchcock, through deception and the danger of getting caught. And apparently out of nervousness – 'I didn't ever want to be at a loss before the actors or the camera crew' – he followed Hitchcock's lead in the extraordinary lengths he took to plan the entire picture ahead of time. 'I made drawings of every set-up through the whole picture from beginning to end. . . . I showed the pictures and drawings to Willy Wyler' (for whom he had written such classics as *Jezebel*)

and he criticized them, and whatever ideas he had I incorporated if they seemed to be good. Before I went on the set Henry Blanke, the producer, gave me the best advice I ever had. . . . Each scene, as you go to make it, is the best scene in the picture . . . the most important. There's no such thing simply as as man getting out of a car door and going into a building. It's got to be made into a scene.

They [the studio] helped me marvellously with the casting. When a director came on a picture at Warners he was given a good deal of authority and the fact that I was the director allowed me to call the shots so far as the actors were concerned. That is, if they were available . . . why, they had a commitment with George Raft, who was a big star at that time, and he was famous for being difficult. . . . Well, he turned down the picture because he didn't want to do it with an unknown inexperienced director, which I can't blame him for at all. So, I thanked God when I got Bogart! I got Bogart and Sydney Greenstreet and Mary Astor. I've never had a better cast.

Huston launched his and Bogart's career with a classic of what would later become known as 'film noir' and with it gave a major career boost for nearly everyone involved. It was the first of the six films he would make with Bogart.

DIRECTOR: John Huston

SCREENPLAY: John Huston

PHOTOGRAPHY: Arthur Edeson

MUSIC: Adolph Deutsch

LEADING PLAYERS: Humphrey Bogart, Mary Astor, Gladys George, Peter Lorre, Barton MacLane, Lee Patrick, Sydney Greenstreet, Ward Bond, Elisha Cook Jr

PRODUCTION COMPANY: Warner Bros

COUNTRY: USA

DATE: 1941

LA DOLCE VITA

The film portrayed the 'sweet life' of Roman society along the Via Veneto, a life of orgies, nightclubs, parties, indulged in by the children of the postwar society who had more money and time than they knew what to do with.

As such, its depiction of morals was a direct challenge to the Catholic Church in its heartland. Based on Fellini's story *Moraldo in Citta*, the film caused its biggest ideological stir as a bone of contention between the left wing in Italy and the Catholic Church, which pronounced the film 'unsuitable for all'. The matter was raised in the Italian Parliament, and even split the Church itself when the Jesuits of the Centro San Fedele came out in support of it. *La Dolce Vita* was described as an 'apocalyptic fresco of seven nightmarish nights and seven sobering dawns', and went on to create a box-office sensation around the world.

Fellini shrugged off the criticism and said,

I presented the problem forcefully. But am I to be expected to offer remedies? Am I a saint, or the Pope, or a head of state? Let spiritual shepherds and social reformers take care of that. I have merely recorded my views. Besides this was not meant to be a socially didactic picture, but a kind of fairy-tale, à propos of a social phenomenon.

It won the Cannes Film Festival prize and the New York Critics award for the Best Foreign Language Film of 1961.

Besides hotting up the tourist trade for Rome, as everyone wanted to share in the 'good' times, Fellini also created a character whose name would become synonymous with a profession: in the film, Mastroianni's sidekick on his rounds of Rome was Paparazzo, a relentless 'photo-reporter' whose name has since entered the language to describe the insatiable hounds of publicity yapping at the heels and feeding off the rich and famous.

DIRECTOR: Federico Fellini

SCREENPLAY: Fellini, Tullio Pinelli, Ennio Flaiano, Brunello Rondi

PHOTOGRAPHY: Otello Martelli

MUSIC: Nino Rota

LEADING PLAYERS: Marcello Mastroianni, Yvonne Furneaux, Anouk Aimée, Anita Ekberg, Alain Cluny, Annibala Ninchi, Magali Noël, Lex Barker, Nadia Gray

PRODUCTION COMPANY: Riama Film/Pathé Consortium Cinéma

COUNTRY: Italy/France

DATE: 1959

Resnais' *Hiroshima Mon Amour* and Truffaut's *Les 400 Coups* shared top honours at the 1959 Cannes Film Festival, but while the judges felt a sense of personal familiarity and affection for Truffaut, the International Critics Prize that went to Resnais was more a gesture of admiration for his 'Left-Bank' politics and his modernist tendencies. There is indeed little which is affectionate about *Hiroshima Mon Amour* though it is in part a love story; just as there is little factual about it though it is in part a documentary; just as it documents with excoriating detail the horrors of the atomic bomb though it is in fact a work of fiction.

The film was written in nine weeks by Marguerite Duras. Resnais wanted to create a work of 'cinematic poetry' on the subject of the atomic bomb. He had already completed his famous documentary, *Night and Fog*, about the concentration camps and wanted to complete his statement with a film about that other horrifying invention of the Second World War. The film is divided between footage shot in Japan and that shot in France. To ensure contrast, Resnais had a Japanese cameraman shoot the Japan footage, which the French director of photography was never allowed to see.

Originally *Hiroshima Mon Amour* was conceived as a documentary, but Resnais found the form too limiting for his ends. Samy Halfron, the producer, suggested a screenplay by Francoise Sagan, but she turned it down. Resnais gave it instead to Duras, whose novel *Moderato Cantabile* he had been impressed by.

Resnais and I both agreed that we could not imagine a film about Japan which did not deal with Hiroshima [Duras recalled], and we also felt that it could be done along the lines of showing the horror of Hiroshima by the scenes of horror that had been done – and very well done – by the Japanese themselves in Children of Hiroshima. *So I tried to do something different. . . . All Resnais said was 'Don't worry about me, forget the camera. Write literature, write as if you were doing a novel.' His idea was to film my scenario just as a composer would set a play to music.*

Film maker Pierre Kast agrees that 'Resnais didn't ask Marguerite Duras for a piece of second-rate literary work meant to be "turned into a film," and conversely she didn't suppose for a second that what she had to say, to write, might be beyond the scope of the cinema. . . .'

And Eric Rohmer, in the same 1959 *Cahiers du Cinema* editorial discussion says, 'To sum up, Alain Resnais is a cubist. I mean that he is the first modern film-maker of the sound film.'

DIRECTOR: Alain Resnais

SCREENPLAY: Marguerite Duras

PHOTOGRAPHY: Sacha Vierny, Michio Takahashi

MUSIC: Giovanni Fusco, Georges Delerue

LEADING PLAYERS: Emmanuele Riva, Eija Okada, Bernard Fresson, Stella Dassas, Pierre Barbau

PRODUCTION COMPANY: Argos/Como/Daiei/Pathé

COUNTRY: France/Japan

DATE: 1959

ROMA, CITTÀ APERTA

ROME, OPEN CITY

Begun in 1944, before the war was over, this was the story of the Italian Resistance leader Don Morosini, a priest who was shot by the Germans.

Federico Fellini was running a series of Funny Face shops – drawing caricatures, taking photographs, mainly recordings for the American soldiers towards the end of the war.

One day Rossellini appeared on the other side of the window, he signalled to me to come outside. He wanted to make a documentary about Don Morosini, who had been shot by the fascists. I agreed rather doubtfully and that documentary became Rome, Open City. *I made a single contract in which I agreed to produce Rossellini's film and a cartoon [these were the Italian comics illustrated with photos for which live actors played out the scenes] about the adventures of a jeep, for the sum of 10,000 lire.*

Rossellini also wanted Fellini to help him persuade Aldo Fabrizi to play Don Morosini.

The film started as a short documentary on 19 January 1944 and was being financed by a wealthy old lady, but as the film expanded she agreed to finance a second film about the activities of Roman youth against the Germans during the occupation. Fellini, and Sergio Amadei, one of the other writers, suggested to Rossellini that the two films should be fused into one.

It was all shot on location – because the studios were destroyed by the war, of course – with mostly non-professional actors in many of the roles and who, fresh from the events, identified spontaneously with their characters.

While shooting in a former gambling saloon near a *maison close*, they were watched by an American officer leaving the 'house'. He offered to place the film in America and actually sold it to an independent distributor.

Despite a surfeit of Resistance films, *Rome, Open City* was received as a genuine work of art. And it marked the beginning of the careers of two of Italy's most famous director-auteurs, and as significantly, that of Anna Magnani, the greatest actress of the Italian cinema.

DIRECTOR:	Roberto Rossellini
SCREENPLAY:	Sergio Amidei, Federico Fellini, Roberto Rossellini
PHOTOGRAPHY:	Ubaldo Arata
MUSIC:	Renza Rossellini
LEADING PLAYERS:	Aldo Fabrizi, Anna Magnani, Marcello Pagliero, Vito Annicohiarico, Nando Bruno
PRODUCTION COMPANY:	Excelsa Minerva
COUNTRY:	Italy
DATE:	1945

The first American film Welles directed since *Macbeth* in 1948 – and the last, all his remaining directorial efforts and the greater part of his acting work being done on the continent. This baroque, brooding tale with the spectacular opening tracking shot that lasts for three minutes was shot in the Southern California coastal town of Venice.

In the same way that Welles the director surrounded himself with a photographer like Russell Metty and a composer like Henry Mancini, so Welles the actor surrounded himself with a wonderful personal cast – Joseph Calleia, Akim Tamiroff, Ray Collins, Dennis Weaver, Mercedes McCambridge, Joseph Cotten, Zsa Zsa Gabor and, in the last 'great' role of her career, Marlene Dietrich.

She was Tanya, the Mexican whore with the German accent, a pianola in her back room and the last and best line in the movie: in response to the previous comment, as Welles lies dying,

"Too bad. He was a great detective but a lousy cop."

Tanya gives his epitaph:

"He was some kind of man."

A film where form overtook content, it is generally acknowledged as being the final film in the Film Noir genre, which started with *The Maltese Falcon*.

Originally released at 95 minutes by Universal, the later version lasts 105 minutes.

DIRECTOR: Orson Welles

SCREENPLAY: Orson Welles

PHOTOGRAPHY: Russell Metty

MUSIC: Henry Mancini

LEADING PLAYERS: Charlton Heston, Orson Welles, Janet Leigh, Marlene Dietrich, Akim Tamiroff, Joseph Calleia

PRODUCTION COMPANY: Universal-International

COUNTRY: USA

DATE: 1958

L'AGE D'OR

THE GOLDEN AGE

Possibly the greatest surrealistic film, and probably the last – in other words, something quite unique.

Conceived as a sequel to *Un Chien Andalou* and first titled 'La Bête Andalouse', it was directed by Luis Buñuel from his own script, with some contributions by Salvador Dali. (The Dali contributions seem to have finally resulted in just one gag – the man strolling with a stone on his head. Dali said in his book *Secret Life of S.D.*: 'I was frightfully disappointed. The film was only a caricature of my ideas. Catholicism was attacked in a primitive, quite unpoetic way.)

Financed by Vicomte de Noailles (who also financed Cocteau's *The Blood of a Poet*), it was filmed in one month at the Billancourt–Epinay Studios. On its premiere in Paris, the cinema was attacked by demonstrators who threw stink bombs and destroyed paintings by Dali, Man Ray and Max Ernst.

It was a witty, yet at the time very scabrous, attack on the Catholic Church, the target for Buñuel in all his films of merit; and it defended the idea of 'free love'. As a result, after some three months of screenings and following a sustained campaign in the right-wing press, the film was banned and all copies of the film were seized by the police. It was not widely distributed for many years in some countries; 1980 in USA and Britain (although there were festival screenings before).

The film has some of the most extraordinary scenes ever to be shot in the history of movies and which have become famous: the girl sucking the toe of the statue, the Archbishop turned into a skeleton with all the others, Gaston Modot destroying the girl's room, the cow on the girl's bed, the history of the scorpions.

They way Buñuel used sound in *L'Age d'Or* was highly original – a cow bell is carried over to the next scene which has the barking of dogs on it; then both sounds are carried over to third scene which returns to the woman with the cow on her bed.

'For the first time in my life I had the impression that I was watching a film which was pure cinema and nothing but cinema.' Henry Miller

DIRECTOR: Luis Buñuel

SCREENPLAY: Luis Buñuel, Salvador Dali

PHOTOGRAPHY: Albert Dubergen

MUSIC: Georges Van Parys

LEADING PLAYERS: Gaston Modot, Lya Lys, Max Ernst, Pierre Prevert

PRODUCTION COMPANY:

COUNTRY: France

DATE: 1930

After the great success of his 1925 film, *Du Skal aere din Hustru (Thou Shalt Honour Thy Wife)*, director Carl Dreyer was invited to come up with a subject that would be suitable for a prestigious art film with which his producers could break into the international market. Dreyer suggested one of three French women of history, Marie Antoinette, Catherine dé Medici, and the Maid of Orléans, the medieval peasant girl who led France to victory against the British and who was burnt at the stake in 1431.

Once it had been just the French but soon she caught the Christian imagination and finally, four hundred years later, in 1920 she was canonized by the Pope. There wasn't a better known or more popular saint than Joan at the time. Her trial and the events surrounding it had been the inspiration for a recent world-wide successful play by George Bernard Shaw, and ten years earlier, a major action-packed film about her had been a significant step in the conversion of the young American director Cecil B. de Mille to a career dedicated to religion and spectacle on the screen.

A film about Joan had therefore a lot going for it as a serious as well as a hugely popular entertainment. But Dreyer chose to ignore the spectacle of history and the romance of battle. Dreyer's film is what writer-turned-director Paul Schrader later described as 'the spiritual progress of Joan's soul'. Dreyer conveys it by concentrating his script (which he began with Joseph Delteil) totally on her trial.

It needed a director of fanatical integrity to overcome the unique problem he had set himself, of creating a profoundly spiritual experience out of Joan's demoniacal persecution by her ecclesiastical judges, questioning her, trying to trick her, twisting her reasons with words, all this in a medium without sound.

Dreyer resolved this through the most eloquent device of the cinema, the close-up. He created, in essence, a gigantic assemblage of close-ups. Joan's trial, her demoniacal judges, her exhaustion and confession and recantation of her forced confession, their sentencing, the shearing off of her hair and her burning at the stake, are almost all shot in close-up. The British critic Tom Milne called the film, 'a symphony of faces'. Dreyer himself said:

I did not study the clothes of the times and things like that. The year of the event seemed as inessential to me as its distance from the present. I wanted to interpret a hymn to the triumph of the soul over life. Everything human is expressed in the face, as the face is the mirror of the soul.

For his Joan he found a young, French, light, boulevard comedy actress, Renée Falconetti. A surprising choice. Later, Dreyer declared, 'Behind the make-up, behind the pose and that ravishing modern appearance, there was something. There was a soul behind that facade.' Her intensely spiritual performance in his film had already proved him right.

To achieve this expressive symphonic eloquence it was essential that none of the cast wore make-up and the panchromatic film stock made their facial details stand out with extraordinary clarity, almost as if etched in relief; an effect that is heightened by shooting them against apparently brilliant white walls – although, in fact, the interior sets were tinted yellow and the exteriors pink so that Dreyer's cameraman Rudolph Mate could achieve this precise sense of brilliance. From first to last, this road to Golgotha aims for and reaches spiritual heights.

DIRECTOR: Carl Dreyer

SCREENPLAY: Carl Dreyer, Joseph Delteil

PHOTOGRAPHY: Rudolph Maté

LEADING PLAYERS: Maria (Renée) Falconetti, Eugène Silvain, Maurice Schutz, Michel Simon, Antonin Artaud, Ravet, André Berley, Jean d'Yd

PRODUCTION COMPANY: Société Générale des Films

COUNTRY: France

DATE: 1927

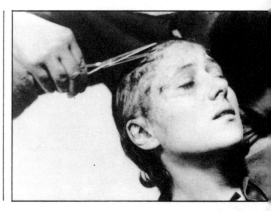

THE SEVENTH SEAL

DET SJUNDE INSEGLET

The title of Ingmar Bergman's morality play, drawn from his own play, *Sculpture in Wood*, which had also been the subject of a radio play, was taken from the Book of Revelations of St John the Divine. The idea for the film, set in medieval Sweden during the plague, was drawn from medieval frescoes showing Death playing chess with his victims. Here it is the knight, who returns home after a crusade (Max von Sydow in the role which was almost to type-cast him, as the director's alter ego, a pained, tortured man bearing all the sins of the world on his shoulders), accompanied by his squire (Gunnar Bjornstrand), cynical and realistic. The innocent couple with their baby, Mia and Jof (Mary and Joseph), a sort of holy family unaffected by thoughts of death and the hereafter, unaware of the stakes and immune from the plague as they frolic in the woods, were cast with other actors who would become famous as the Bergman stock company.

Bergman himself described *The Seventh Seal* as 'a modern poem, presented with medieval material that has been very freely handled. The knight of the film returns from a crusade, as a soldier in our times returns from a war.'

This film, coming close on the heels of his earlier comedy, *Smiles of a Summer Night*, both of which were honoured at the Cannes Film Festival, established him as a director of international repute.

DIRECTOR:	Ingmar Bergman
SCREENPLAY:	Ingmar Bergman
PHOTOGRAPHY:	Gunnar Fischer
MUSIC:	Erik Nordgren
LEADING PLAYERS:	Gunnar Bjornstrand, Bengt Ekerot, Nils Poppe, Max von Sydow, Bibi Andersson, Inga Gill
PRODUCTION COMPANY:	Svensk Filmindustri
COUNTRY:	Sweden
DATE:	1956

'**I**'m always a bit offended when I hear that one of my films is "auto-biographical": it seems like a reductionist definition to me, especially if then, as it often happens, "autobiographical" comes to be understood in the sense of anecdotal, like someone who tells old school stories.'

Yet, Amarcord means 'I remember' in the Roman dialect and the source material clearly comes from *La Mia Rimini*, a bit of memoir by Fellini in which many of the real characters who turn up in the film first appear. Perhaps the best way to approach *Amarcord* is as a fanciful memory, a virtually plotless escape back to what was, what might have been, perhaps what should have been.

Be careful, [says Fellini] 'Amarcord' doesn't mean 'I remember' at all; . . . it is a word of seduction, the brand of an aperitif. . . . I wanted to call it simply Viva Italia! *Then I thought this would have been too mysterious or too didactic. Another title I wanted to give it was* Il Borgio, *in the sense of a medieval enclosure.*

Amarcord is the third of a trilogy begun with *The Clowns* and *Roma* – the latter also recreated in a studio. With the exception of Magali Noel, all the cast were non-professionals or came from the music hall and provincial theatres. (The small town in *Amarcord* refers back to *I Vitelloni* and looks forward to *And the Ship Sails On* in the magical scene with the ocean liner.)

As ever, Fellini assembled his usual panoply of odd and memorable characters, setting them up in a series of comic vignettes – some might call them gags – that become a pastiche of life in a small Italian village as seen through the eyes of a young boy on the edge of innocence and puberty. His *Amarcord*, whether autobiographical or not, won Fellini the Oscar for Best Foreign Film.

DIRECTOR: Federico Fellini

SCREENPLAY: Fellini, Tonino Guerra

PHOTOGRAPHY: Giuseppe Rotunno

MUSIC: Nino Rota

LEADING PLAYERS: Puppela Maggio, Magali Noel, Armando Brancia, Ciccio Ingrassia

PRODUCTION COMPANY: F C Produzioni/PECF

COUNTRY: Italy/France

DATE: 1973

Mizoguchi's film from the novel by Ogai Mori is a tale of suffering and self-sacrifice set in eleventh-century Japan. The title refers to the sadistic Bailiff Sansho who systematically persecuted, tortured and ruined a once proud and prosperous noble family. The portrayal of their persecution is given in scenes both of barbaric violence and of extremely subtle visual delicacy.

There are slow dissolves, a few close-ups, and wonderful, almost translucent photography by Kenzuo Miyagawa, master of the tracking shot, skills he had already demonstrated to great effect in Kurosawa's *Rashomon*. Nature, majestically beautiful and immutable, is very prominent in the film, almost more than in any other Japanese movie. Against a gliding background of haunting beauty – played mostly on or near water, which, as with John Ford's use of the desert in *The Searchers*, serves both to lock people in and to shut them out – life goes on in harrowing detail.

Writing in the wake of his discovery of the film, Adrian Turner found the use Mizoguchi makes of the camera

painterly, – electing set-ups which convey the emotional and physiological essence of a situation with none of the contrivance that flaws much of John Ford's work and certainly none of Ford's cloying sentimentality. Mizoguchi's cinema is dynamic and obsessively fluid; his tracking and crane-shots have a naturalism that one rarely encounters elsewhere. . . . Form and content are indivisible.

Mizoguchi, born in Tokyo in 1898, was originally a painter, kimono designer and newspaper layout artist before turning to films in 1920. He directed his first film in 1922 and completed over 90 features before his death in 1956.

DIRECTOR: Kenji Mizoguchi

SCREENPLAY: Yahiro Fuji, Yoshikata Yoda

PHOTOGRAPHY: Kazuo Miyagawa

MUSIC: Fumio Hayasaka

LEADING PLAYERS: Kinuyo Tanaka, Yoshiaki Hanayaki, Kyoko Kagawa, Eitaro Shindo, Akitake Kono, Masao Chimizu, Ken Mitsuda, Kazukimi Okuni

PRODUCTION COMPANY: Daiei

COUNTRY: Japan

DATE: 1954

L'AVVENTURA

Speaking about Neo-Realism, Antonioni commented that in the 1950s the social and economic realities of war-devastated Italy had, in effect, been normalized. Using *Bicycle Thieves* (1948) as an example, he continued, 'the problem of the bicycle had been eliminated. It was no longer necessary to show the conditions which had given rise to the theft, and the time had now come for a less sentimental, more objective treatment of post-war Italian life.'

In *L'Avventura*, his most derided, talked about, and ultimately artistically successful film, more than bicycles had been eliminated. It was the movie that was different. The relationship of surface actions to the deeper meaning are like shadows on sculptures. What occurs beneath the surface is all. *L'Avventura* can be seen to come out of Rossellini's *Viaggio in Italia*, though Antonioni creates his own star (Monica Vitti), and in a sense, this tradition reaches its apotheosis in Resnais' *L'Année Dernière à Marienbad*, though that French puzzle is all surface glitter with none of the psychological depth of the Italian experience. But the clues, the plot, what there is of it in these films the way one knows it, are minimal. At the start, the cast is there, in Naples, a castle in Bavaria, or, as in *L'Avventura*, positioned around the grey Sicilian landscape.

Early in the film a young woman, Anna, disappears/dies/possibly having committed suicide during a short boating holiday. Her lover, Sandro, and her friend, Claudia, become lovers. Halfway through, the dead woman is forgotten. Her body is never found and the people who are looking for her aren't part of the story. Feelings appear to be on the emotional level of one of Andy Warhol's Campbell soupcans, or how one might react to it. During a party aboard the boat the wife of one man allows herself to be groped by one of the other guests and neither she nor anyone else there seems to notice or care.

During its premiere at the 1960 Cannes Film Festival, the film, its director and star were greeted by the international assembly of their peers and film distributors with a fusillade of catcalls and slow hand-claps. It was the

DIRECTOR: Michelangelo Antonioni

SCREENPLAY: Antonioni, Elio Bartolini, Tonino Guerra

PHOTOGRAPHY: Aldo Scavarda

MUSIC: Giovanni Fusco

LEADING PLAYERS: Gabriele Ferzetti, Monica Vitti, Lea Massari, Dominique Blanchar

PRODUCTION COMPANY: Cino Del Duca/Prod. Cinematografiche Europee, Société Cinématographique Lyre

COUNTRY: Italy/France

DATE: 1959

public, not the film, that had got out of hand. Four months later, and wiser, it was awarded the London Film Festival's prize for, 'the most original and imaginative entry to be shown'. Antonioni was to have been present here as well but he was detained in Rome after the Italian authorities seized the film and banned it for being obscene. (The publicity helped.)

When it came to the United States *Time* magazine called it 'a nightmarish masterpiece of tedium'. Insecure exhibitors, fearing that they might have a loser on their hands, quoted the review but left out the last two words.

Yet, long after the shock of the new has died away, even thirty years later, people who saw it remember it as a landmark in their experience: for its strong atmosphere, its hypnotic quality and for a depth of feeling unique in films, then as now. At the Cannes press conference Antonioni stated: 'The conclusion at which my characters arrive is not moral anarchy. They come, at the most, to a kind of shared pity. This, you may say, is nothing new. But without that, what is left to us?'

Buster Keaton's masterpiece – the peak of silent comedy – was based on a true incident recalled by William Pittinger in his Civil War story, *The Great Locomotive Chase* (the title and basic plot were used for the 1956 Walt Disney children's film). The film had a strong storyline: Pittinger had been one of a band of twenty sent to seize the rebel-run locomotive known as *The General*. Keaton had hoped to shoot the film in the original Alabama Tennessee terrain, but when this proved impossible as no narrow gauge tracks remained, it was shot in Oregon. Two locomotives were converted into outward replicas of *The General* and *The Texas*. He hired two regiments of the Oregon State Guard, who helped to put out the forest fire started by sparks from *The General*.

The gags, when they come, are built on the principle of surprise to the hero, or to the audience, and often on situations in which only the audience knows what has happened on the track ahead, or, for instance, when the sword with which Keaton struggles flies out of the scabard to impale the enemy sniper.

The film has less than fifty titles and a happy ending, unlike the one in real life, where the train thieves were some nineteen miles away from their safe rendezvous.

DIRECTOR: Buster Keaton, Clyde Bruckman

SCREENPLAY: Al Boasberg, Charles Smith

PHOTOGRAPHY: Bert Haines, J. D. Jennings

LEADING PLAYERS: Buster Keaton, Marian Mack, Glenn Cavender, Jim Farley, Frederick Vroom, Charles Smith, Frank Barnes, Joe Keaton, Mike Donlin, Tom Nawm

PRODUCTION COMPANY: United Artists

COUNTRY: USA

DATE: 1927

LIFE OF O-HARU

SAIKAKU ICHIDAI ONNA

As a child Kenji Mizoguchi witnessed the sale of his elder sister into the life of a geisha, an event which was to have a profound influence on his work. Jonathan Rosenbaum wrote, *O-Haru* 'is a depiction of woman treated, traded, valued, degraded and discarded as material object'.

It is the story, based on a famous literary work, *Koshuku Ichidai Onna (The Life of a Woman Who Loved Love)*, telling of the waning fortunes of the daughter of a rich merchant and is set in seventeenth-century Japan. She eventually ends up as a prostitute and the film is a very fine example of the director's interest in the victimization of women in feudal Japan. Kinuyo Tanaka, who took the leading role, was one of Japan's outstanding actresses, and later became Japan's first woman film director. Her life was recreated in Kon Ichikawa's 1987 film, *The Actress*, which has a complete full-scale reconstruction of the final sequence from *The Life of O-Haru*.

Mizoguchi had a particularly hard time getting this film made, and had to work in very difficult conditions, shooting in a disused armament factory, after the producers, Shintoho, refused him its studios. He was 56 and near the end of his career when he won international recognition and the Silver Lion for this work at the 1952 Venice Film Festival.

DIRECTOR: Kenji Mizoguchi

SCREENPLAY: Yoshikata Yoda

PHOTOGRAPHY: Yoshimi Hirano

MUSIC: Ichiro Saito

LEADING PLAYERS: Kinuyo Tanaka, Ichiro Sugai, Tsukie Matsuura, Toshiro Mifune

PRODUCTION COMPANY: Shin Toho

COUNTRY: Japan

DATE: 1952

LE CHARME DISCRET DE LA BOURGEOISIE

THE DISCREET CHARM OF THE BOURGEOISIE

The title proved to be a problem – Buñuel himself came up with 'A bas Lenine, ou la Vierge à l'écurie' (Down with Lenin, or the Virgin in the Manger), only on the last day of shooting. Then someone suggested 'Le Charme de la Bourgeoisie', which he liked but knew it needed an adjective and tried many before settling on *discret*.

The theme of the film was the impossibility of satisfying a simple desire, one that often occurs in his films. Here it is the characters' wish to try and eat dinner together.

Buñuel wrote in his autobiography,

One day when my producer and I were talking about uncanny repetitions, he told me the story about the time he invited some people for dinner but had forgotten to tell his wife. In fact, he forgot that he'd been invited out to dinner himself that same evening. When the guests arrived he wasn't there; his wife was however, but in her bathrobe, and since she had no idea anyone was coming, she'd already eaten and was about to go to bed. This incident became the opening scene of Discreet Charm and from there we repeated the patter, inventing all sorts of situations. The script went through five different versions while we tried to combine realism – the situation had to be familiar and develop logically and the accumulation of strange, but not fantastical obstacles. Once again dreams helped, particularly the notion of a dream within a dream. (I must confess too, how happy I was to be able to include my personal recipe for the dry martini.)

The Discreet Charm of the Bourgeoisie won the 1972 Oscar for the Best Foreign Language Film.

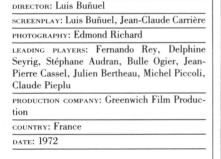

DIRECTOR: Luis Buñuel

SCREENPLAY: Luis Buñuel, Jean-Claude Carrière

PHOTOGRAPHY: Edmond Richard

LEADING PLAYERS: Fernando Rey, Delphine Seyrig, Stéphane Audran, Bulle Ogier, Jean-Pierre Cassel, Julien Bertheau, Michel Piccoli, Claude Pieplu

PRODUCTION COMPANY: Greenwich Film Production

COUNTRY: France

DATE: 1972

NAPOLÉON

Although made in 1925, the film used everything we think of as being used or developed later in cinema, i.e. colour, superimposition, slow motion, split screen, the camera as snowball, the camera attached to a horse to get sense of involvement.

The film used Polyvision and screen tryptich – which Gance defined thus: 'The theme, the story one is telling, is on the central screen. The story is prose and the wings, the side screens, are poetry.'

First released two years after its production, 1929 – in America astonishingly in a 70-minute version – trade paper *Variety* said, 'Film doesn't mean anything to the great horde of picture goers over here.' Then a sound version, edited by Gance, was reissued in 1935 and dialogue was added to a further version in 1955. In 1971, a 13-reel sound version was released under the patronage of Claude Lelouche. Finally, Kevin Brownlow's restored version saw the light of day in 1979.

Abel Gance's *Napoléon* is probably a film which has gained more importance on account of its reconstruction than by what it is – although technically it was well in advance of its time, the personal and human element in it are rather lacking.

Ultimately, its appeal is probably due to the way it conveys a sense of the historical importance of the characters and events.

DIRECTOR: Abel Gance

SCREENPLAY: Abel Gance

PHOTOGRAPHY: Jules Kruger, Jean-Paul Mundwiller, L. H. Burel

LEADING PLAYERS: Albert Dieudonne, Gina Manes, Edmond Van Daele, Alexandre Koublitzky, Acho Chakatouny, Antonin Artaud, Marguerite Gance, Abel Gance, Annabella

PRODUCTION COMPANY: Westi/Société General des Films/Les Films Historique

COUNTRY: France

DATE: 1927

THE SACRIFICE

OFFRET SACRIFICATIO

The issue I raise in this film [explains Tarkovsky] is one that to my mind is most crucial. The absence in our culture of room for a spiritual existence. We have extended the scope of our material assets and conducted materialistic experiments without taking into account the threat posed by depriving man of his spiritual dimension. Man is suffering, but he doesn't know why. He senses an absence of harmony, and searches for the cause of it.

The film is a poetic parable. . . . I am well aware that it is a film at variance with the prevailing ideas of our time. . . . But need I point out that I am a believer, and that I am astonished by the spiritual (and by no means only spiritual) suicide that we are rushing toward, even though no regime is forcing us to it? . . .

I never managed to separate my life from my films, and I have always had to make crucial choices. Many directors manage to live one way and express other ideas in their work; they are able to split their conscience. I am not. To me cinema is not just a job. It's my life.

Of the work of this Russian artist, Ingmar Bergman said,

My discovery of Tarkovsky's first film was like a miracle. Suddenly, I found myself standing at the door of a room the keys of which had, until then, never been given to me. It was a room I had always wanted to enter and where he was moving freely and fully at ease.

I felt encouraged and stimulated: someone was expressing what I had always wanted to say without knowing how. Tarkovsky is for me the greatest, the one who invented a new language, true to the nature of the film, as it captures life as a reflection, life as a dream.

DIRECTOR: Andrei Tarkovsky

SCREENPLAY: Andrei Tarkovsky

PHOTOGRAPHY: Sven Nykvist

LEADING PLAYERS: Erland Josephson, Susan Fleetwood, Valerie Mairesse, Allan Edwall, Gudrun Gisladottir, Sven Wollter

PRODUCTION COMPANY: Swedish Film Institute/Argos

COUNTRY: Sweden/France

DATE: 1986

LE NOTTI DI CABIRIA

CABIRIA NIGHTS OF CABIRIA

The critic Dilys Powell observed that, 'Fellini's heroine (a little street-walker) has nothing to do with either viciousness or romantic pity' (the usual designation for the screen's *women of the night*). Cabiria, played by Giulietta Masina

is a scruffy little creature absurdly dressed in ankle-socks and mangy fur, who is buying her house . . . who is born to be bilked and puts a brave face on it. Matter-of-fact and comically truculent, her exercise of her job is observed against the background of professional gossip and the faintly sinister farce of professional rivalry.

The wardrobe which Cabiria and the others wore was bought by Fellini at the Porta Portese street market – after all, the director was still, at this point, regarded as a neo-realist.

The story went round at least ten different potential producers, including a Swiss financier who was ready to make the film until he discovered in the last three pages that Cabiria does not get married.

Pier Paolo Pasolini wrote the dialogue for the 'Divine Love' part. Shooting lasted four months in the summer and autumn of 1956, including a delay of 50 days when Masina fractured her knee. The film won Fellini the director's prize and the Oscar for Best Foreign Film of 1957, and became the inspiration for a popular American musical *Sweet Charity* (Fellini's *8½* was the source for another of Broadway's finest musicals of recent years, *Nine*) and the brilliant directorial film debut of the stage's choreographer and director, Bob Fosse).

DIRECTOR: Federico Fellini

SCREENPLAY: Fellini, Ennio Flaiano, Tullio Pinelli

PHOTOGRAPHY: Aldo Tonti, Otello Martelli

MUSIC: Nino Rota

LEADING PLAYERS: Giulietta Masina, Amadeo Nazzari, François Perier Fellini

PRODUCTION COMPANY: Dino de Laurentiis/Films Marceau

COUNTRY: Italy/France

DATE: 1957

THE THIEF OF BAGDAD

There never has been a more wonderful, more ravishing fairy-tale put on the screen by anyone, anywhere, that so beautifully pays tribute to the magic of the cinema itself. Made at the outbreak of the Second World War, it was the realization of producer Alexander Korda's dream to dazzle and uplift.

Michael Powell, one of the three directors credited on the titles (the others were Ludwig Berger and Tim Whelan, though over the period of 20 months it took to make, both Alex and Zoltan Korda and production designer William Cameron Menzies took turns at helping out) recalled:

Korda realised that he wasn't going to get the film he wanted [from Berger who had started it]. So he sent for me and said, 'I want you to start on some sequence down in the Cornwall with Sabu and the ship wreck and the bottle, go to work them out with the crew.' Vincent Korda would go away and build a set. [Bagdad, Basra, bazaars and palaces, harbours, minarets and temples in the sky, all that one associates with Orientale] Alex would come and look at it and say, 'Vincent, you're crazy! Go away, get a lot of men, build it four times as big and paint it all crimson. It stinks.' And Vincent would ram his hat over his eyes and go off and that was how The Thief was built up colourwise. [The film won Oscars for colour photography, colour art direction and special effects.] Paradoxically, it is almost impossible to see something approximating the original Technicolor.

The film was begun in England and finished in America. War broke out while they were there, and Korda moved the production to California. There were two sets of supporting actors, and three directors; during the shooting the Indian and Pakistani extras playing Medes and Persians came up against Alex's usual problems, a shortage of funds and went on strike against unfair wages.

The day would eventually come when Alexander Korda could no longer pay his bills but by the time of his death, a grateful British nation had made him a knight.

DIRECTOR: Ludwig Berger, Michael Powell, Tim Wheland

SCREENPLAY: Lajos Biro, Miles Malleson

PHOTOGRAPHY: Georges Perinal, Osmond Borradaile

MUSIC: Miklos Rozsa

LEADING PLAYERS: Conrad Veidt, Sabu, June Duprez, John Justin, Rex Ingram, Miles Malleson, Morton Selten, Mary Morris

PRODUCTION COMPANY: London Films

COUNTRY: GB

DATE: 1940

T hat *The Navigator* was ever made was a combination of chance and the seemingly boundless resourcefulness of Buster Keaton. Fred Gabouri, a friend of Keaton's, had been hired to find old out-of-commission sailing clippers that might be dressed up to look like Elizabethan war vessels for *The Sea Hawk*. Keaton, meanwhile, had given up work on a project that required the use of a cruise ship that was to have this plot line by Jean Havez: 'I want a rich boy and a rich girl who never had to lift a finger. . . . I put these two beautiful, spoiled brats – the two most helpless people in the world – adrift on a ship alone. A dead ship. No lights. No steam.' But, unfortunately, Keaton also had no ship to use in the filming.

That was when Fred Gabouri, on his search for clippers, found a derelict he knew was perfect for the film Keaton was proposing. 'I told you a long time ago,' he said to Keaton, 'that I'd get you a real boat. Well I've got you a real honest-to-God ocean liner. You can do anything you please with her – sail her, burn her, blow her up, sink her.' Work on the film began immediately.

Comparisons with Chaplin's *Modern Times*, made over ten years later, abound, and in fact there are distinct parallels in the idea of man against machine. But Keaton was also concerned about the relationship to the young lady, also stuck on board the ship:

There we were in the dead of night, floating out to sea, neither one of us knowing the other was aboard. There was a lot of discussion, should we be strangers or not? My idea was that we should know each other and have a mutual problem. Marooned together – or shanghaied by fate you might say – the problem would really be sitting in our laps. Only then, you see, we'll have a bigger problem – no two-bit problem who marries who, but just staying alive on a derelict ship.

Clyde Bruckman, one of the script writers, later talked about the end of the film:

DIRECTOR: Buster Keaton, Donald Crisp
SCREENPLAY: Jean C. Havaz, Joseph A. Mitchell, Clyde Bruckman
PHOTOGRAPHY: Elgin Lessley, Byron Houck
LEADING PLAYERS: Buster Keaton, Kathryn McGuire, Frederick Vroom, Noble Johnson
PRODUCTION COMPANY: MGM
COUNTRY: USA
DATE: 1924

We were trying to shake the pattern of the final chase. A hard thing to do, it was set in the public mind. 'The Chase,' Buster was always saying, 'is just one form of climax. It works so well because it speeds up the tempo, generally involves the whole cast, and puts the whole outcome of the story on the block.'

The Navigator was hugely successful. Grossing over $2 million (in 1924!), it had cost only $211,000 to make. This included $25,000 for the fuel, crew and rental of the ship, and an expensive underwater scene, the shooting of which epitomized Keaton's willingness not only to put money into his projects but to put himself through every kind of physical torment in the pursuit of his comedy. The scene, set on the ocean bottom under the ship, was actually shot in Lake Tahoe so early in the season that Keaton could only stay underwater in his diving suit a few minutes at a time. The cameraman, sitting in a specially constructed diving bell, had to wear arctic gear.

ORDET

THE WORD

Ordet has been called the 'ultimate black-and-white film, the one that says it all'. Dreyer's use of whites and greys have inspired critics and audiences to find metaphysical, theological concepts within the 'colour' scheme alone. This, along with a mysterious, yet naturalistic sense of movement – as in the birth sequence when the doctor's motions are in complete sympathy with the very pulse of life – ranks *Ordet* among the most technically sophisticated of films.

Yet Dreyer himself spoke more of *Ordet's* inner life:

Regarding the history and cultural impact of the religious conflict present in Ordet, *I was so much happier doing* Ordet *when I felt myself very close to the conceptions of Kaj Munk [the playwright on whose play the film is based]. He always spoke well of love. I mean to say, of love in general, between people, as well as love in marriage, true marriage. For Kaj Munk, love was not only the beautiful and good thoughts that can link man and woman, but also a very profound bond. And for him there was no difference between sacred and profane love. Look at* Ordet. *The father is saying, 'She is dead . . . she is no longer here. She is in heaven . . .' And the son answers, 'Yes, but I loved her body too . . .'*

It was a theme to which Dreyer would return in his last great work *Gertrud*.

DIRECTOR: Carl Dreyer

SCREENPLAY: Carl Dreyer

PHOTOGRAPHY: Henning Bendsten

MUSIC: Paul Schierbeck

LEADING PLAYERS: Henrik Malberg, Emil Hass Christensen, Preben Lerdorff Rye, Cay Kristiansen, Birgitte Federspiel, Ejner Federspiel, Sylvia Eckhausen, Gerda Nielsen

PRODUCTION COMPANY: Palladium Film

COUNTRY: Denmark

DATE: 1954

Ken Kesey, the main character in Tom Wolfe's *The Electric Kool-Aid Acid Test*, was himself the author of the book that inspired the play which Kirk Douglas bought in 1963 and wanted to make but grew too old so that his son eventually produced it and Jack Nicholson played it thirteen years later in 1975. Kesey never saw the film. Nor does he intend to. The reason he wouldn't, he claimed, was that they had bastardized his story. When he wrote his book he used his LSD experiences to describe what would happen to the inmates in the asylum when they were forced to take prescription drugs to keep their metabolism under control. He considered this a major part of his story. Yet, the film's Czech director Milos Forman, still new to America, would have none of this sixties drug culture:

The character in the book through whose eyes the story is told is a schizophrenic and at the beginning is very much under the influence of drugs. All that psychedelic, hallucinatory stuff in films, I just don't like it anymore. I thought the film primarily had to be realistic, then entertaining.

(Forman, having won the Oscar for his direction, went on to make the dire film version of one of the most psychedelic of the sixties rock-operas, *Hair*.)

The main character (Nicholson won the Oscar for playing Randal McMurphy) was doing time for brawling and statutory rape, 'She was fourteen going on 35', when he decides to feign madness in the misguided belief that a nut house would be a better place to stay in than a state penitentiary.

DIRECTOR: Milos Forman

SCREENPLAY: Lawrence Hauben, Bo Goldman

PHOTOGRAPHY: Haskell Wexler

MUSIC: Jack Nitzche

LEADING PLAYERS: Jack Nicholson, Loiuse Fletcher, William Redfield, Will Sampson, Brad Dourif, Christopher Lloyd, Danny De Vito

PRODUCTION COMPANY: Fantasy Films

COUNTRY: USA

DATE: 1975

But the state lunatic hospital becomes a symbol for America and the struggle of the oppressed individual against the system. Systems, as we all know, do not cater to the individual.

On its release, the public, reacting to some extent against the American system that had wilfully prolonged the agony of Vietnam, made the film the most successful movie in the history of United Artists, and, in that frame of emotion, it swept the Oscars. Nicholson told *Time Out*,

Making the film I got very depressed at first because it was hard to comprehend that you can't talk to someone. I've had to reason with a lot of people who I think are eccentric and I never have any problems with them. But when you're talking to someone who has killed people, molested or just sat in a closet and counted his shirts for a month, you just don't feel like you're on a one to one basis. I started talking to the people who worked in the hospital about what it was like being exposed to that. Of course they had a very obvious answer which was that people do get out, every week, every month, every day, who never come back. So that's the sort of way I coped with that.

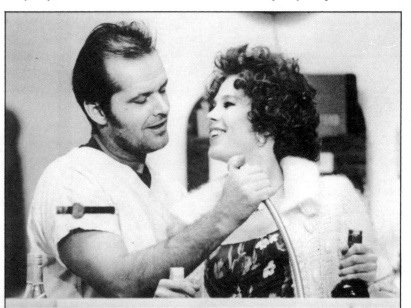

Andrzej Wajda had already directed *Kanal* and *A Generation* when he brought Jerzy Andrzejewski's novel *Ashes and Diamonds* to the screen under the strict censorship that prevailed in Cold War Poland, and made a film that has been praised for its sense of new ideas and creative freedom.

The film, like the novel, takes place in one day and night, and is set almost all in the hotel in town.

In part, its success on the international scene – it won the Critics Prize in Venice in 1959, as well as, and perhaps more significantly, in his native Poland – had to do with the casting of Zbigniew Cybulski as Maciek. In his dark glasses and costume he sums up a whole generation of rebels of 1950 – although the events were set in postwar Poland.

Jerzy Andrzejewski said, 'during the writing of the book, I pictured Mack Chelmicki entirely differently. Now when I see the film, I see him only . . . as Cybulski played him.'

The James Dean of Poland – Zbigniew Cybulski may have been an unpronounceable name in most of the world, but there are women who have developed a sudden passion for linguistics in order to pronounce his exotic

DIRECTOR: Andrzej Wajda

SCREENPLAY: Andrzej Wajda, Jerzy Andrzejewski

PHOTOGRAPHY: Jerzy Wojcik

LEADING PLAYERS: Zbigniew Cybulski, Ewa Krzyzanowska, Adam Pawlikowski, Waclaw Zastrzezynski

PRODUCTION COMPANY: Kadr Unit, Film Polski

COUNTRY: Poland

DATE: 1958

consonants, and young men everywhere copied his famous black glasses which were in fact light green, but they photographed black. *Time* magazine profiled the actor in 1964. The impact of his personality – which more than the film transcended cultural and language barriers – meant that Andrzej Wajda found it impossible to work with him again: 'Since I offered him such an outstanding role in *Ashes and Diamonds*, it was very difficult later to find something appropriate to match the image.' Wajda's reasoning is curiously like the explanations given by a lot of other directors – from Griffith to Lilian Gish, von Sternberg to Marlene Dietrich – when Galatea becomes bigger than Pygmalion.

A compact tale, and a complex one, the film it concerns the attempt by members of the nationalistic underground, who resent the new Communists nearly as much as they did the Nazis, to murder the new Communist District Secretary. Wajda explained how he managed to make a film of such intentionally divided sympathies under the nose of the censors:

What you have to do is to try to make every scene so fit with the ideology of the film that there is very little individually for the censor to cut. There were two different things they wanted to cut out, for example, the final scene in the garbage dump. Luckily they didn't succeed. This was basically not censored because of the way that Cybulski played the role – though in the circumstances of those days when the film was being made, the character that Cybulski played was negative. Because he is . . . aiming to shoot the Communist. But the moment he actually plays it the way he does – he's such a nice guy – you cannot censor it. After that the rest follows. I mean what in particular are you going to cut out – the scene where he laughs? There is nothing to cut out. And that's the real problem in making a movie and fighting the censor.

Roman Polanski, who had appeared in the first film of the trilogy, *Kanal*, had wanted to make a film based on the macho legend of Cybulski revolving around nine of the actor's erotic relationships, to be shot in only nine takes, in the style of Hitchcock's *Rope*. Though nothing has come of it.

SENSO

WANTON CONTESSA

The film, derived from short stories by Camillo Boito, was published for the first time in Boito's *More Vain Stories* in 1883. The author had actually been pointed out to Luchino Visconti when the director was a young boy. *Senso* told of the Venetian countess Livia's love affair with the young Austrian officer Franz Mahler during the last months of Italy's revolt against its Austria masters. The Italian uprising culminated in the Battle of Custoza, which had been his original idea for the title. Though it was only given a couple of lines in textbooks Visconti felt it to have been of great importance to Italy. It was a period in his country's history and a time of momentous change to which he would return again years later with *The Leopard*. Italy's Austro-Germanic connections would also resurface in several of his other, later works, *The Damned* and *Ludwig II*. And, as with *Death in Venice*, which utilized Gustav Mahler's music, so *Senso* used Bruckner's Seventh Symphony to great effect.

First choice for Livia ('the [so-called] wanton countess' which its American distributors called it in the hopes of reaching a larger public) was Ingrid Bergman, but her husband Rossellini would not let her go.

Visconti had wanted Marlon Brando for Franz Mahler but Lux Film, who couldn't have afforded Brando, insisted on Farley Granger who gave the best performance of his career.

Pressure was put on Visconti by a number of parties including the producer, the Italian Minister of Defence, and the censor, who objected to the political line of the dialogue, especially to the strongly emphasized antagonisms between the patriots, led by Giuseppi Garibaldi, and the regular army. Furthermore, the original ending of the film, where Franz's tale was uncertain, was cut and the negative burned. Film was shown at Venice Film Festival in 1954 where a considerable part of its artistic success was Visconti's first-time use of colour aided by the superb photography of Robert Krasker, Giuseppe Rotunno and, Aldo Graziati (who was killed during the shooting).

Visconti said, 'After *Senso*, everything was easier.'

DIRECTOR: Luchino Visconti

SCREENPLAY: Luchino Visconti, Suso Cecchi d'Amico, Giorgio Bassani, Giorgio Prosperi, Carlo Alianello, Paul Bowles, Tennessee Williams

PHOTOGRAPHY: G. R. Aldo, Robert Krasker, Giuseppe Rotunno, Aldo Graziato

MUSIC: Bruckner's Seventh Symphony

LEADING PLAYERS: Alida Valli, Farley Granger, Massimo Girotti, Heinz Moog, Rina Morelli, Marcella Mariani, Christian Marquand

PRODUCTION COMPANY: Lux Film

COUNTRY: Italy

DATE: 1954

This was Tarkovsky's testimony to the past.

In Mirror, *I am treating for the first time a subject which literally tells a lived story.* So that creates a fear of evoking personal sensations which will then be judged at the tribunal of the spectators. It corresponds to the moment when one forces oneself to talk. Is one right in making the spectator watch one's personal problems? Is it certain that a story of this kind can express something general?

This was Tarkovsky's testimony to the past. With this film Tarkovsky again took up the theme of childhood and the family, the mirror representing a fragmented autobiography. 'It's the story of my mother and thus a part of my own life. The film contains only genuine incidents. It's a confession.'

Tarkovsky was much concerned with recalling the separation of his parents in 1935 – the poems by his father, Arsney Tarkovsky, are read by the son and superimposed on the images of the young boy in the film. It was a highly personal reminiscence from a director who was not at all in favour of or in favour with the authorities. When the film was finished it was placed in Category 3 (the Russian equivalent of the American art-house circuit) which meant that it only had a limited release, being shown in a few out-of-the-way suburban Moscow cinemas, and it was criticized for being obscure by the Union of Soviet Cinematographers. A typical reaction came from Grigori Chukhrai, the director of *Ballad of a Soldier*, 'One must not orientate oneself to some special kind of audience. Cinema art is an art of the masses. And if the artist has something to say he doesn't put his thoughts into code, he says what he thinks.'

DIRECTOR:	Andrei Tarkovsky
SCREENPLAY:	Andrei Tarkovsky, Aleksandr Misharin
PHOTOGRAPHY:	Georgy Rerberg
LEADING PLAYERS:	Margarita Terekhova, Philip Yankovsky, Ignat Daniltsev, Oleg Yankovsky, Innokenti Smoktunovsky
PRODUCTION COMPANY:	Mosfilm Unit 4
COUNTRY:	USSR
DATE:	1974

More than likely, if any of the key personnel involved in the making of this picture, both behind and in front of the camera, had been asked to name their favourite of their films, this would have been the one. One cannot ignore the emotions that engendered it; the time in which it was made (just after the war); and the honours with which it was heaped, 9 Academy Awards in America, and many from abroad. It was a film made and bathed in a spirit of proud humility and thankfulness, as Wyler, directing his first film since he left the forces, and his writer and the rest of the best crew Samuel Goldwyn's money could put together, recreated the postwar experiences of a group of American veterans (a middle-aged sergeant, an airforce officer and a sailor who has lost both hands) returning to their homes and families, their wives and children, and their new place in society.

So why then is this honoured and honourable film a bit like going to church instead of like going to the movies? Church can be nice but you know you're going to get a sermon, and when American directors launch into heartfelt sermons on the big screen it's hard to ignore that they were probably paid a fortune for their sincerity.

There is no doubt that *The Best Years of Our Lives* was sincere about all the emotions it thawed out in the public of the time, no question that it is as superb a piece of American film craftsmanship as, for example, *Casablanca* or *Meet Me in St Louis*, or any of the earlier films directed by William Wyler whose meticulousness on a film was legendary and who would do take after take until he was sure the scene was right. As he told Myrna Loy, who played the wife she had by then been playing so long and so well, 'If we do it again something special may happen.' This 'special' in too many of Wyler's films is the thoroughly applied polish so that it glows with the dignity of hard work. But wax browns wood, it doesn't turn plywood into pine.

So, with time, over forty years since it was made and released – long enough for the sentiments with which it was received to have been handed on to other 'returning soldiers from the front' films, and the same cheers and the same awards given to *Coming Home*, and *Platoon* – what there still is about *Lives* is what it was. It's good.

And there is the now lost joy to be found in an almost documentary innocence which allowed the people of a nation to believe that everything their government said and told them to do was the truth and right. Those really were the best years of their lives.

DIRECTOR: William Wyler

SCREENPLAY: Robert Sherwood

PHOTOGRAPHY: Gregg Toland

MUSIC: Hugo Friedhofer

LEADING PLAYERS: Fredric March, Myrna Loy, Teresa Wright, Dana Andrews, Virginia Mayo, Cathy O'Donnell, Hoagy Carmichael, Harold Russell

PRODUCTION COMPANY: Samuel Goldwyn

COUNTRY: USA

DATE: 1946

For its title alone one could treasure such a film. And this late flowering Nouvelle Vague critic-turned-director's films are as enchanting as the landscapes in which he sets them, as radiant as the amateurs he blends in so adroitly with his mature professionals and they contain a sting as subtle as that of a late summer breeze whose cooling fragrance twists and bares the first currents of autumn in its sensuous stroke. *Le Genou de Claire*, the fifth of Rohmer's *contes moraux*, as Jan Dawson observed, 'scrutinises the behavioural niceties of a mature man resolved to commit his life to the woman he loves, meeting temptation in her absence, resisting it and abiding by his original decision'.

Eric Rohmer, a founding member of France's New Wave, writing for *Cahiers du Cinema* for ten years, editing it from 1957 to 1963, was already past fifty before he too began to make films. His first two films, *Signe du Lion* and *Paris Vu Par*, were shorts shot on 16mm. *La Collectionneuse* and the greatly applauded *Ma Nuit chez Maud* were features that made him one of the most talked about directors on the international scene. By the time of *Le Genou de Claire*, things had become more sophisticated.

He still had Nestor Almendros, one of the foremost cinematographers of his age, working with him; and he had the money for colour and leisure. Colour was important.

The sense of time – evening, morning, and so on – can be rendered in a much more precise way through colour. Colour can also give a stronger sense of warmth, of heat, for when a film is in black and white you get less of a feeling of the different moments of the day, and there is less of what you might call a tactile impression about it. In Le Genou de Claire I think it works in the same way: the presence of the lake and the mountains is stronger than in black and white. . . . The colour green seems to me essential in that film. I couldn't imagine it without green in it. And the blue too – the cold colour as a whole. This film would not have value for me in black and white. It's very difficult to explain this.

DIRECTOR: Eric Rohmer

SCREENPLAY: Eric Rohmer

PHOTOGRAPHY: Nestor Almendros

LEADING PLAYERS: Jean-Claude Brialy, Aurora Cornu, Béatrice Romand, Laurence de Monaghan, Michèl Montel, Gérard Falconetti, Fabrice Luchini

PRODUCTION COMPANY: Les Films du Losange

COUNTRY: France

DATE: 1970

The tale told is of an elegant 35-year-old diplomat, whose fondness for young girls seems to be realized when he summers at Lake Annecy with its rich vegetation and surrounding mountains. While there a chance reunion with a Romanian novelist leads him to the family with whom she is staying, and the two half-sisters there – 16 and 17. He is pursued by the elder but it is Claire, the younger, who excites his interest. Nothing 'happens' – thinking about it is most of it, and the major event is when he succeeds in putting his hand on her knee. Yet the charm is enormous. I'm reminded of something the British playwright J. M. Barrie once said – that there are certain situations where, if you have charm you need nothing else, and if you don't have it, nothing else is of much help. Rohmer achieves his 'charm' with his articulate, literary script, his settings, his observation and his marvellous mix of professionals and amateurs. On the one hand he chose Jean-Claude Brialy because the actor seemed very close in fact to the character of Jerome. On the other hand he chose Aurora Cornu for the Romanian novelist who seems to orchestrate the events of the film as if they might be characters in a novel she could be writing because Cornu is, indeed, a Romanian novelist.

EARTH

ZEMLYA

According to John Howard Lawson, 'No film artist has ever surpassed Alexander Dovzhenko in establishing an intimate human connection between images that have no plot relationship.'

Rob Edelman writes, 'The storyline of *Earth*, Dovzhenko's . . . greatest film (he wrote the screenplay in a matter of days), is deceptively simple: a peasant leader is killed by a landowner after the farmers in a small Ukrainian village band together and obtain a tractor. But these events serve as the framework for what is a tremendously moving panorama of rustic life and the almost tranquil admission of life's greatest inevitability: death. Without doubt, *Earth* is one of the cinema's few authentic masterpieces.'

The images of earth, nature, life giving birth, ripening, falling, healing and repeating the process are unforgettable. In its famed opening sequence, which Dovzhenko based on the memory of his grandfather's death, a mesme-

rically tranquil effect is created by the absolute, uncluttered isolation of the images. Ukrainian wheat fields ripple in magnificent undulating long-shot, apples hang from the trees. Nature and humanity are combined within the frame. Dawn: ploughing, reaping, winnowing and dough-making. At the end, apples are dashed by the life-giving rain; the downpour ceases; a single apple is shown in extreme close-up.

The poetic nature of the film wins out over the obvious political propaganda of the story. It was controversial in its day and Russian critics condemned it as politically incorrect because its lyricism overrides the storyline and fails to place the major emphasis on specific events and struggles relating to the Revolution. Dovzhenko wrote, 'I was so stunned by the attacks, so ashamed to be seen in public, that I literally aged and turned grey overnight. It was a real emotional trauma for me. At first I wanted to die.'

After its Russian premiere, he brought the film to Paris and Berlin. The film created a sensation outside the Soviet Union. Its simple imagery influenced other directors, particularly documentary filmmakers in England and the United States, where it opened in the fall of 1930. In its own but remarkably similar way, one is reminded of Peter Weir's film, *Witness*, about a simple, rustic American community interrupted momentarily by outside events, but which ultimately draws its power and pure beauty, not from the senselessness of human actions, but from the land, and its celebration of life.

DIRECTOR:	Alexander Dovzhenko
SCREENPLAY:	Alexander Dovzhenko
PHOTOGRAPHY:	Vasili Krichevsky
LEADING PLAYERS:	Semyon Svashenko, Stepan Skhurst, Iou Sointseva, Mikola Nademsky, Yelena Maximova
PRODUCTION COMPANY:	Ukrainfilm
COUNTRY:	USSR
DATE:	1930

Visconti's second full-length film was almost a documentary. Inspired by the work of Giovanni Verga, it deals with the battle the fishermen wage with nature, with conscription, oppression from the rich, death and, above all, the Fates. Originally planned as a three-part investigation about the social problems in that part of Italy (the other two were to have been about mining and agriculture), it was shot entirely on locations in Aci Trezza, a fishing port in Sicily, with a cast of non-professionals.

It would have been impossible [said Visconti] to obtain from even the finest actors the truthfulness and simplicity of Sicilian fishermen – but it was perfectly possible to get Sicilian fishermen to express their own genuine feeling in their own surroundings and circumstances. One often hears talk of 'actors picked off the street'. This seems to me a contradiction in terms. It would be very difficult to transform fishermen into professional actors after years of work. . . .

However, although seemingly spontaneous, and an early classic of Italian neo-realism, the film, as with all of Visconti's subsequent work, is a model of style and organization. With a team of about eighteen people (including the 25-year-old Francesco Rosi and Franco Zeffirelli) doing the work of sixty or seventy, Visconti was able to keep expenses to a minimum. He not only wrote the script but, with conductor Willy Ferreo, he composed the music from traditional Sicilian airs.

DIRECTOR: Luchino Visconti

SCREENPLAY: Luchino Visconti

PHOTOGRAPHY: G. R. Aldo

MUSIC: Visconti, Willy Ferrero

LEADING PLAYERS:

PRODUCTION COMPANY: Universalia, Rome

COUNTRY: Italy

DATE: 1948

DAS KABINETT DES DR CALIGARI

THE CABINET OF DR CALIGARI

The story is based on a true-life episode witnessed by the Czech, Hans Janowitz, one of the authors of the film, who was strolling in the Reeperbahn fairground, looking for a young girl who had caught his attention. He followed her into a dim park, where he glimpsed a shadowy figure in the dark. The next day the papers reported a sex crime in the park; the young girl had been killed. He went to her funeral and seemed to sense the presence of the murderer.

The other theme came from co-author Carl Mayer's experiences while being examined by a high-ranking military psychiatrist during the war. The two men came together and they wrote a manuscript over a period of six weeks. They came across the name of the central protagonist in *The Unknown Letters of Stendhal*, in which the author told about his meeting with an officer named Caligari at La Scala.

The director Robert Wiene introduced the framing device of having the story told through the madman's fantasy, although the authors were furious at the change. A large degree of the film's impact and its reputation ever since was attributable to its expressionistic settings, which were designed by one of the forerunners of surrealism, Alfred Kubin. The painted two-dimensional sets are openly cubist, gothic, and have a theatrical visual style, a world of slanting walls, crooked chimneys, and windy, convulsively twisted passages and doors, suggesting an atmosphere of menace and madness, and dictating the performances of the players.

Ironically, considering the importance given by critics to the chiaroscuro effects, the recent showings of the original version reveal it to have been heavily tinted in greens, browns and steely blues, which gives the film an even more dramatic aspect, notably in the framing madhouse scenes where blue and green, mixed to considerable artistic effect, create a definite haunted quality that clearly separates these scenes from the madman's fantasy and clarifies the plot.

The film played continuously in the same Paris movie house from 1920 to 1927, a record only beaten by *Emmanuelle* in 1974.

DIRECTOR: Robert Wiene

SCREENPLAY: Carl Mayer, Hans Janowitz

PHOTOGRAPHY: Willy Rameister

LEADING PLAYERS: Werner Krauss, Conrad Veidt, Friedrich Feher, Lil Dagover, Rudolf Klein-Rogge

PRODUCTION COMPANY: Decla Bioscop

COUNTRY: Germany

DATE: 1919

The film consists of six episodes situated in various parts of Italy, and follows the progress of the Allied Armies from south to north. The initial episode, which Rossellini had only roughly worked out, was adapted to the two actors they found by chance. Fellini, who with Massimo Mida worked as Rossellini's assistant director, described the situation:

We were surrounded by a whole new race of people, who seemed to be drawing hope from the very hopelessness of their situation. There were ruins, trees, scenes of disaster and loss, and everywhere a wild spirit of reconstruction. In the midst of which we did our tour. The troop of people working on Paisà *travelled through an Italy they scarcely knew, because for twenty years, we'd been in the grip of a political regime which had literally blindfolded us.*

The impact of this film, along with the earlier *Open City*, cannot be underestimated. The Taviani brothers saw the film after school one day.

They were showing Paisà. *Everybody in the half-empty room was protesting the film. The public was rejecting what for us two was a shock; to find on the screen that which we had just left on the streets. We finally ended up getting into a fight with some of the spectators. Our decision was made: we understood what we wanted to do with our lives. The cinema.*

It was then that Fellini also realized that his true occupation could only be that of a film director. 'When I weighed up my laziness, my ignorance, my curiosity, my lack of discipline and my incapacity to make sacrifices, I convinced myself that the cinema was my vocation.'

In New York, Ingrid Bergman saw the film in 1948.

So he'd made another great movie! And nobody had ever heard of him! I looked down the theatre. It was almost empty. What was going on? This man had made two great films and he was playing to empty houses. I think it was at that moment that the idea came to me. Maybe, if this man had someone who was a name *playing for him, then maybe people would come and see his pictures. . . . And this immense feeling grew inside me that movies like this simply* must *be seen by millions, not only by the Italians but by millions all over the world. So, I thought, I'm going to write him a letter.*

Paisà won a collective prize at Venice, the National Film Board of Review's best film of 1948, and the New York Film Critics Best Foreign Film award, and Ingrid Bergman made her fateful *Viaggio in Italia*.

DIRECTOR:	Roberto Rossellini
SCREENPLAY:	Federico Fellini, Roberto Rossellini, Sergio Amidei
PHOTOGRAPHY:	Otello Martelli
MUSIC:	Renzo Rossellini
LEADING PLAYERS:	William Tubbs, Gar Moore, Maria Michi
PRODUCTION COMPANY:	OFI/Capitani/Foreign Film Productions
COUNTRY:	Italy
DATE:	1946

CASQUE D'OR

B efore becoming a director Jacques Becker had worked as an assistant to Jean Renoir for eight years. The influence of Renoir is clear in this, his only period film. Becker stated that he was aiming for 'something between the writing of Eugene Sue and the paintings of Auguste Renoir'. That is, he tried to blend the lurid quality of Sue's novels with the open sensuality of Renoir's pictures. In this he was notably aided by fine atmospheric black and white photography and evocative art direction. It also benefited enormously from one of the finest performances given by Simone Signoret, who won the British Academy Award for Best Foreign Actress as the golden-haired Marie, a courtesan who falls for the young carpenter (Serge Regianni). Signoret said, 'In the course of exercising my craft, *Casque d'Or* was a turning point. I discovered that basically you know nothing about this craft, and there is nothing to learn. As one ages, one needs less and less of its science. I feel a real need not to think, not to analyse.'

DIRECTOR: Jacques Becker

SCREENPLAY: Jacques Becker, Jacques Companez

PHOTOGRAPHY: Robert Le Febvre

MUSIC: Georges Van Parys

LEADING PLAYERS: Simone Signoret, Serge Reggiani, Claude Dauphin, Raymond Bussière, Gaston Modot, Paul Barge

PRODUCTION COMPANY: Speva/Paris-Film

COUNTRY: France

DATE: 1952

As the last of the classic surrealists of the screen [wrote Andrew Sarris] Buñuel . . . improved with age. What once seemed simple and obvious about his art has been purified by a stylistic serenity. Where he was once merely profane, he is now eminently profound.

In this film, made in 1962, Buñuel dealt with the bourgeoisie as sheep who cannot leave the Church.

Angel is full of repetitions, some twenty of them in fact: guests enter the room twice, people either meet themselves or are introduced to the same person three times, the same toast is offered and then offered again, the soirée – as in the film itself – ends as it began, with piano music. And the characters say, to emphasize the point, 'In everyday life we repeat ourselves every day.'

Buñuel himself, as if defying order and reason even when discussing the film, said,

As to the ending, there is really no logical explanation. The Exterminating Angel is like a plague. First it starts with a small group of people, then a whole church full, then on to the rest of society. The revolution is just a mass outburst of the society which the forces of order try to put down. But the fact is that, whether they wanted to or not, the society is in a fix. I guess that is about the only 'symbolic' interpretation one could give.

DIRECTOR: Luis Buñuel

SCREENPLAY: Luis Buñuel

PHOTOGRAPHY: Gabriel Figueroa

MUSIC: Scarlatti

LEADING PLAYERS: Silvia Pinal, Jacqueline Andere, Augusto Benedico, Luis Beristain, Antonio Bravo, Claudio Brook, Cesar del Campo, José Baviera

PRODUCTION COMPANY: Gustavo Alatriste

COUNTRY: Mexico

DATE: 1962

MANHATTAN

Manhattan almost makes you want to move to New York. Woody Allen, most of whose films have been set there, has a love affair going with the Big Apple. He described it as a 'romantic comedy about the tendency for marriage to collapse and the American culture to decline, the terrible influence of television, the bane of drugs and fast food and the inability of people to take control of their lives'. Woody Allen is a comic genius. He tends to answer philosophical questions about *Why?*, like, 'Why did he make this movie?' and 'What does it mean?' with his movies. He is unique. For the past two decades he has been the most consistently great American film director working.

Like Stanley Donen's homage to Paris in *Funny Face*, Woody's hymn to his native Manhattan also makes its case to the music of Gershwin – 'Rhapsody in Blue'; 'Love Is Sweeping The Country'; 'S'Wonderful'; 'Lady Be Good'; 'Strike up the Band'; and 'Embracable You'. The film was shot by his usual cameraman in impeccable black and white, but the emotions are in colour. Like Fellini and Bergman, Allen also has the rare knack of making the most unlikely actresses great and the Great American Nerd into a viable intellectual sex symbol. 'Is Manhattan still a dream city to you? I get angry and frustrated when I think of it, but it's the same kind of frustration that you get when someone you love disappoints you. But in *Manhattan* I'm not critical of New York: I question the roots of it. It's not a movie that says "Clean up Central Park". It's a movie that says "Clean up your emotional life or you'll never be able to clean up Central Park".'

On the nights of the Oscar ceremonies in Hollywood, Woody Allen, who is inevitably nominated, and often a winner, can be found in a small jazz club in his native Manhattan playing his clarinet.

DIRECTOR: Woody Allen

SCREENPLAY: Woody Allen, Marshall Brickman

PHOTOGRAPHY: Gordon Willis

MUSIC: George Gershwin

LEADING PLAYERS: Woody Allen, Diane Keaton, Michael Murphy, Mariel Hemingway, Meryl Streep, Anne Byrne

PRODUCTION COMPANY: United Artists/Rollins-Joffe

COUNTRY: USA

DATE: 1979

The setting, visually striking, is a huge icy baroque hotel, 'a world of marble and stucco, columns, mouldings, gilded ceilings, statues; a world of servants, frozen stiffly in their place'. The garden is as formal. (The film was shot in Bavaria in the palace of Nymphenburg and the park at Schleissheim.) Wandering through and around are the guests, 'anonymous, civilised, unmistakably rich and idle, serious but dispassionately observing the rules of the games they play, of the dances they dance, the chit they chat of their pistol shooting excursions'.

Within this stifling world everyone seems to be under a spell, as in those French fairy-tales where time stands still and everyone waits for a prince to kiss the princess so that the rest of them can get on with their own business. The main protagonists are a girl (known only as A, Delphine Seyrig), an older man who appears to be her husband (M), and another man, seemingly a stranger (X), who claims to have started an affair with her last year at Marienbad. The film offers no apparent clues: it does not differentiate between what seems to be happening now and what may have happened then, between real and imagined, memory and fantasy.

'I'd like anyone who sees it to interpret it in terms of its meaning to him,' Alain Resnais has said. 'It's not a "fixed" work of art. I'd like to make films which can be approached from all kinds of angles, as one looks at sculpture.'

Then, suddenly, she is ready to yield.

Like Rubic's cube, the film became a craze, a drawing-room event, something else to talk about besides the weather. Film festivals vied for it. At Venice it won the 1961 Grand Prix. It's hard to remember it now, or to care, except for its images, of human penguins and swans in a garden, of A leaning against X, or looking at M, or resting her marble cheek on a statue's marble foot, and so recalling, for an instant, an image from Buñuel.

DIRECTOR: Alain Resnais

SCREENPLAY: Alain Robbe-Grillet

PHOTOGRAPHY: Sacha Vierny

MUSIC: Francis Seyrig

LEADING PLAYERS: Delphine Seyrig, Giorgio Albertazzi, Sacha Pitoeff

PRODUCTION COMPANY: Terra/Tamara/Cormoran/Precitel/Como/Argos/Cinetel/Silver/Cineriz

COUNTRY: France/Italy

DATE: 1961

75 MY DARLING CLEMENTINE

The film was Ford's last as a contract director for Fox, the company he had worked for since 1921.

Wyatt Earp, one of the central figures of Old West mythology who died in 1928, had spent much time hanging around the movies, instructing friends and young directors like John Ford, on how to tell his story. His life was turned into a book by Stuart Lake, *Wyatt Earp – Frontier Marshal*. Four films would be based on it: *Frontier Marshal* (1934), *Frontier Marshal* (1939), *My Darling Clementine*, and *Powder River* (1953).

Wyatt Earp's (Henry Fonda) shave in Tombstone is disturbed by a drunken Indian, Joe (Charles Stevens). The title refers to Clementine Carter (Cathy Downs), who becomes the town's first schoolmarm, and is wooed by Earp. Yet the true heroic figure, in the Ford sense, is Doc Holliday (Victor Mature) whose dignity and sense of responsibility, and eventual martyrdom, echoes characters in other Ford classics – Casey in *Grapes of Wrath*, Brickley in *They Were Expendable* and Tom Doniphon in *The Man Who Shot Liberty Valance*. But Wyatt is the glamorous central figure: attractive, elegant, perfumed, and impeccably dressed.

Ford, who, like others, may have been misled by the self-romanticizing Earp about the true nature of his deeds remembered:

About Clementine, *the only story I know is, Wyatt Earp moved out here and lived some place beyond Pasadena and his wife was a very religious woman, and two or three times a year . . . she'd go away on these religious conventions, Wyatt would sneak into town and get drunk with my cowboys. Along about noon they'd sneak away and come back about one-fifteen swacked to the gills – all my cowboys and Wyatt, and I'd have to change the schedule around. And he told me the story of the fight at the O.K. Corral. So in* My Darling Clementine, *we did it exactly the way it had been . . . except that Doc Holliday was not killed. Doc died of tuberculosis about eighteen months later. . . . the finish of the picture was not done by me. That isn't the way I wanted to finish it.*

DIRECTOR:	John Ford
SCREENPLAY:	Samuel Engel, Winston Miller
PHOTOGRAPHY:	Joseph P. Macdonald
MUSIC:	Cyril J. Mockridge
LEADING PLAYERS:	Henry Fonda, Linda Darnell, Victor Mature, Walter Brennan, Tim Holt, Ward Bond, Cathy Downs, Alan Mowbray, John Ireland, Grant Withers, Jane Darwell
PRODUCTION COMPANY:	20th Century-Fox
COUNTRY:	USA
DATE:	1946

Why not also *Der Blaue Engel*, or *Morroco, Shanghai Express, Dishonoured, Blonde Venus* and *The Devil Is a Woman*? All were directed by Josef von Sternberg and starred Marlene Dietrich, the greatest Pygmalion and Galatea combination in the twentieth century. All are the sublime works of a master and his 'spiritual' mistress. This was the sixth and most expensive of their seven films together and by now the writing was on the box-office walls for audiences had become blinded by so much splendour, jaded by the countless copies made in the wake of Dietrich and his films, and studios were in the business of making films that made money, not 'masterpieces' that didn't return their investment.

It wasn't that von Sternberg had said all there was to say about love, and the nature of love, and of an obsession with love that could lead a man to

ruin and even death (that theme would be tackled in their last work) but, more likely, that audiences were still reeling from the images thrown up by their previous films, and also the fact that changes in America were taking place: the country was working its way out of the Depression and preferred simpler, more optimistic and accessible subjects. Besides, just before the release of this Byzantine epic set in barbaric eighteenth-century Russia about the corruption of an innocent young girl forced into marriage with a despotic halfwit, they had seen the much romanticized British-made version of these same events. As a result the release of *Scarlet Express* was delayed by six months, which killed the momentum.

Of course, as with all his films, the camerawork was stupendous: for Sternberg, the camera, more than words, was his pen, and through it he communicated his ideas. Dietrich, ageing from 16 to 30, was played as a child by her own daughter Maria. Sternberg's control, absolute, even extended to the music: he not only conducted but also arranged the works of Mendelssohn, Wagner and Tchaikovsky. Dietrich is the centre of a work in which every gesture is von Sternberg's and in which every frame, with and without her, is essential to an experience that is cinema at its purest and most dazzling.

DIRECTOR: Josef von Sternberg

SCREENPLAY: Manuel Komroff

PHOTOGRAPHY: Bert Glennon

LEADING PLAYERS: Marlene Dietrich, John Lodge, Sam Jaffe, Louise Dresser, Maria Sieber, C. Aubrey Smith

PRODUCTION COMPANY: Paramount

COUNTRY: USA

DATE: 1934

GREED

Eric Von Stroheim's masterpiece was taken away from him, cut by three-quarters, mutilated almost beyond recognition and yet remains today a brilliant work of art.

The stark drama in which Von Stroheim wished 'to show real life, with its degradation, baseness, violence, sensuality, and a singular contrast in the midst of this filth, purity', he cast almost exclusively with favourite comedy players of the day – Zasu Pitts, Dale Fuller, Chester Conklin, Hughie Mack, Franks Hayes, Tiny Jones. Von Stroheim gave himself a bit part as the balloon seller at the fair.

Von Stroheim began the film in the Goldwyn company and took an unheard of ten months (and $750,000) to shoot *Greed*, the first cut of which was an equally unheard of 42 reels long – the equivalent of 10 hours on screen. Scenes that included gold props, or any sort of gold-related objects, were hand-tinted in the original release prints. Irving Thalberg, who inherited the project when Goldwyn was sold and merged into Metro-Goldwyn-Mayer, ordered him to cut it, and he did, mortgaging his house, car, and life insurance because he was forced to do the work without pay. But Von Stroheim couldn't bring himself to cut it past 24 reels, still a six-hour film. That wasn't good enough for the new studio, and Von Stroheim gave the editing over to his friend Rex Ingram who managed to rein it down to 18 reels. But by this time Thalberg had had enough. He got another editor, who cut the film to an acceptable 2 hours 45 minutes. 'You were ten years ahead of your time,' Billy Wilder once remarked to von Stroheim. 'No,' replied the director. 'Twenty.'

We will never know how much more powerful the remaining footage might have made a different final version. Irving Thalberg, who once cracked that Von Stroheim, whose obsession with women's feet and their foot gear was well known, was a 'footage fetishist', supposedly had ordered the unused film melted down for its silver content.

Greed was a work of great passion for Von Stroheim, the film he had literally dreamed for years of making. At the end of the gruelling shoot, he shouted at two of his actors who were slugging it out in a fight scene, 'Fight, fight! Try to hate each other as you hate me!' Jean Hersholt, who played Marcus, acknowledged that 'In order to get realism, he really would make you hate him.'

Even in its fragmented form, *Greed* inspired a generation. In the Thirties, a group of Russian film teachers visited Hollywood and asked to meet Von Stroheim. 'We show your *Greed* to all our students,' they said to him. 'That, we tell them, is the way.'

DIRECTOR: Erich von Stroheim

SCREENPLAY: Erich von Stroheim

PHOTOGRAPHY: William Daniels, Ben Reynolds, Ernest B. Schoedsack

LEADING PLAYERS: Gibson Gowland, Zasu Pitts, Jean Hersholt, Chester Conklin, Sylvia Ashton, Dale Fuller, Joan Standing, Austin Jewel

PRODUCTION COMPANY: Metro-Goldwyn Pictures

COUNTRY: USA

DATE: 1925

Thin romantic fantasy by Michael Powell/Emeric Pressburger, which Powell described as 'a stratospheric joke told against the background of Two Worlds, photographed in Technicolor and dye-monochrome', launched the first Royal Command Film Performance in 1946. Except for Jack Cardiff, who commenced his brilliant career as a lighting cameraman with this film, Powell surrounded himself with his usual excellent team both in front of and behind the scenes. For a film that set itself a whole set of technical problems for the sheer joy of solving them – freeze frames, moments when the changes from monochrome to colour take place in mid-shot, sets that had to convey a sense of the hereafter and the now below – it was important to have the harmony that comes from having the best ready to carry them out. Michael Powell said that for him

A Matter of Life and Death is the most perfect film, the technical perfection and the fact that it is a most wonderful conjuring trick to get handed. It is all the more fascinating to me because all this fantasy actually takes place in a medical case, inside someone's damaged head (David Niven), so there was a good sound medical reason for every image that appeared on the screen. The film was actually started by the Ministry of Information sending for us and saying, 'Well, the war's nearly over boys, but it's just starting from our point of view. We think you should make a film about Anglo-American relations because they are deteriorating.' Of course they didn't know we would come up with A Matter of Life and Death,

whose underlying theme was that 'the rights of the *uncommon* man must always be respected'. The whole idea was predicated on the romantic notion (and Powell is nothing if not a romantic) that love is more powerful than national boundaries (the British flyer and his American sweetheart), more powerful even than death, for, 'Love is Heaven, and Heaven is love.'

The film was one of a remarkable series of ambitious, highly individual, iconoclastic, decidedly 'un-British', and, inevitably, astonishingly inventive works by this Anglo-Hungarian producer/director/writer team, the likes

DIRECTOR: Michael Powell and Emeric Pressburger

SCREENPLAY: Michael Powell and Emeric Pressburger

PHOTOGRAPHY: Jack Cardiff

MUSIC: Allan Gray

LEADING PLAYERS: David Niven, Kim Hunter, Robert Coote, Kathleen Byron, Richard Attenborough, Marius Goring, Roger Livesey, Raymond Massey, Bonar Colleano

PRODUCTION COMPANY: The Archers

COUNTRY: GB

DATE: 1946

of which had never been seen in the English cinema before or since. Other of their films include *The Life and Death of Colonel Blimp*, *A Canterbury Tale*, *Black Narcissus*, *The Red Shoes* and *The Tales of Hoffman*, my favourite among which, at any one moment, depends on the one that came to mind first. They are all so much of a one.

THE WIZARD OF OZ

This film has acquired enormous sentimental status with Americans who first saw it on TV when CBS bought it for its annual Christmas showings in the late fifties. Like that other yuletide chestnut *It's a Wonderful Life*, Frank Capra's unashamedly maudlin hymn to the 'ordinary' in every 'him', *Wizard*'s present standing in critical esteem has less to do with hidden virtues overlooked on its release (when neither film was much of a critical or popular success) than to the power of the TV medium. *The New Yorker*'s critic had called it 'a stinkeroo'. But for millions of adolescent Americans their early TV exposure to these films, contrasted with the usual made-for-TV fare, was like seeing an action-packed American B-film in post-War Europe. TV gave these 'A'-sized failures a novelty appeal they lacked on release in an era of plenty. (*Oz* has a better excuse for its initial failure since the musical fantasy, a prestige project, cost a staggering $2,777,000; a fortune by pre-Second World War standards.)

The annual TV blitz to which Americans owe the rise of these movies in their esteem resulted from the fact that *Wonderful*, due to an oversight, was out of copyright and cost nothing to show, and CBS bought the rights to show *Wizard* for a derisory amount. Such were the programming incentives. Since then there has even been an expensively produced book about the making of this 1939 MGM technicolour children's classic in which Judy Garland sang *Over The Rainbow* and won a Special Oscar for playing Dorothy, the little girl who left Kansas in a cyclone to learn that there is no place like home.

Wizard was directed by Victor Fleming, a much admired and highly respected studio director with his handsome, well-crafted films that excelled at projecting the appeal of the great stars (Cooper, Gable, Clara Bow, Jean Harlow, Tracy, Bergman). But, whereas it will come as little surprise that Jean Vigo should have two of the only five films he made in his brief life included in surveys like this, one of which, *Zéro de Conduite*, also dealt with a childhood world but minus the sentimentality, it will probably come as a great surprise that Victor Fleming, who directed over forty films between 1919 and his death in 1949, should also crop up, not once but twice, while more highly regarded American directors like Frank Capra, George Stevens, Gregory La Cava, Preston Sturges, Robert Siodmak, or George Cukor aren't included at all. And, as with Michael Curtiz being the director of Warner Brothers *Casablanca*, so it is, dare I say, safe to assume with Fleming's receiving the sole credit for MGM's *Wizard of Oz* and Selznick's *Gone with the Wind*, that any of the omitted directors could have made these three films as well. Even after Fleming replaced Cukor who had started filming *Gone with the Wind*, several other directors worked on the film during its long production, either because Fleming had fallen ill from exhaustion or because Selznick wanted to speed it up. And on *Wizard*, Cukor (again) and Richard Thorpe had done some preliminary work and King Vidor shot some final sequences after Fleming had left to replace Cukor on *Gone with the Wind*. This was the studio way, with which all these men were familiar. Yet Fleming's contribution was essential to both films and his reputation deserved. As highly regarded as a director of male stars (Clark Gable, who modeled his own persona on Fleming, was one of the primary reasons why Fleming was brought into GWTW) as George Cukor was for directing women, Fleming's handling of actresses is less known but one has only to see the range of skilful emotions he brought out in sex-pots

like Clara Bow and Jean Harlow, to see how good he was. And because of his handling of children in *Treasure Island* and *Captains Courageous*, he was entrusted with the tricky problems inherent in filming one of America's favourite children's stories, *The Wizard of Oz*.

Wizard was a fantasy and fantasies were one of Hollywood's big taboos. They lost money. Which was why Samuel Goldwyn, who owned the rights to the Frank Baum books, was willing to sell them to MGM. With ten writers (including Herman Mankiewicz who suggested the transition from black and white to colour before he moved on to *Kane*), four directors, two hundred midgets, six months in production and one million over budget, the special effects were incredible, the songs immortal, Garland (third choice after Shirley Temple and Deanna Durbin) an 'overnight' legend, and all of it a peak of the studio factories' art. The score and the song, 'Over the Rainbow', (which only stayed in by a fluke) won Oscars in 1939. The rest of the awards that year, including Fleming's Oscar for direction, went to *Gone with the Wind*.

DIRECTOR:	Victor Fleming (King Vidor, Richard Thorpe)
SCREENPLAY:	Noel Langley, Florence Ryerson, Edgar Allan Woolf
PHOTOGRAPHY:	Harold Rosson (colour); Allan Darby (black and white)
MUSIC:	Harold Arlen
LEADING PLAYERS:	Judy Garland, Frank Morgan, Ray Bolger, Bert Lahr, Jack Haley, Margaret Hamilton, Billie Burke, Charley Grapewin, Clara Blandick
PRODUCTION COMPANY:	MGM
COUNTRY:	USA
DATE:	1939

Historian William K. Everson believes that, 'It is probably the best of the "man-made monster" genre from any period . . . . In terms of style, visual design, literate scripting, performance, music and nearly every other individual ingredient, it is practically unexcelled.'

Bela Lugosi, who had been the original choice to play *Frankenstein*, after his success with *Dracula*, but had turned it down, giving Boris Karloff the opportunity that would make him the foremost horror household name, was now due to play alongside Karloff as Dr Pretorius, but the part went to English actor, Ernest Thesiger. (Lugosi would finally appear in the third in the series, *Son of Frankenstein*, as the crazed hunchback Ygor.) Elsa Lanchester not only played the monster's bride, but that of authoress Mary Shelley in the prologue. Because of the monster's size she was given elevator shoes and a floor-length gown to hide them.

Franz Waxman's score, a departure from horror films which until then stuck to the classics, became a popular piece of Universal music, resurfacing in numerous films and particularly identified with the *Flash Gordon* serials.

This sequel, unlike most, is generally regarded as being superior to the original. Mel Brooks' excellent 1974 satire, *Young Frankenstein*, re-created the original set.

In a radio interview in 1935, which opened with appropriate electrical sound-effects, Boris Karloff said, 'I shall create a monster like Frankenstein's. No brain – just a huge creature which shall guard against reporters and interviewers. "Connect the electrodes! Throw the switches! It lives! It moves! Karloff's Monster lives!"' When the 'Monster' finally spoke, it was with the voice of his interviewer. 'Alas,' Karloff said, 'I have created a Frankenstein monster. It's a fan-magazine writer.'

DIRECTOR: James Whale

SCREENPLAY: John L. Balderston, William Hurlbut

PHOTOGRAPHY: John D. Mescall

MUSIC: Franz Waxman

LEADING PLAYERS: Boris Karloff, Colin Clive, Valerie Hobson, Elsa Lanchester, Ernest Thesiger, Dwight Frye

PRODUCTION COMPANY: Universal

COUNTRY: USA

DATE: 1935

This was Katharine Hepburn's last film for RKO where she had begun her distinguished career in 1932. *Baby* never did well at the box office, and even Hawks himself (who at the time had made only one comedy, the cyclonic *Twentieth Century* with John Barrymore) later felt that the film had one great fault: every character in it was a screwball. There was no reference point for the audience, no way for them to find the centre. Hawks swore never again to make a comedy in which every last character was crazy. And yet today, audiences seem to agree more with Harold Lloyd who once told Hawks that it was the best constructed comedy he had ever seen, and that, to him, it was a classic.

Bringing Up Baby is indeed a clockwork farce that pushes its characters further and further into ever more embarrassing and humiliating circumstances. Grant, a staid scientist, is put at the mercy of a nutty, fixated heiress (Hepburn), who has taken charge of a tame, but hungry leopard named Baby who can only be subdued by serenading him with 'I Can't Give You Anything but Love, Baby'. Baby disappears, along with a valuable dinosaur bone. Meanwhile a wild leopard escapes from the local zoo, is mistaken for Baby and the rest of the film is a mad chase to retrieve the bone and avoid getting in 'Baby's' way.

Grant himself was reluctant to play the part of the palaeontologist, claiming that he wouldn't know how to play an intellectual; it had already been turned down by Ray Milland, Ronald Colman, and Robert Montgomery. But Hawks convinced him that basing the character on Harold Lloyd would work, and it did – brilliantly. At one point in the script, Grant is called on to make a sound to denote his anger, a sound which must nevertheless be funny to others. He succeeded, again with Hawks' suggestion, in making a noise like a horse whinnying in frustration. Grant would keep the sound in his repertoire, using it again and again in future films (watch *Arsenic and Old Lace*).

Baby was long written off as an ill-conceived venture. Not until recently has it been appreciated for its ruthless humour, technically flawless construction, and the pairing of its two screen legends, Grant and Hepburn.

It has spawned several imitations – most notably in the 1970s, Bogdanovich's *What's Up Doc?* and in the 1980s Madonna's *Who's That Girl?*

DIRECTOR: Howard Hawks

SCREENPLAY: Dudley Nichols, Hagar Wilde

PHOTOGRAPHY: Russell Metty

MUSIC: Roy Webb

LEADING PLAYERS: Katharine Hepburn, Cary Grant, Charles Ruggles, May Robson, Walter Catlett, Barry Fitzgerald, Asta

PRODUCTION COMPANY: RKO

COUNTRY: USA

DATE: 1938

82 IF...

Lindsay Anderson's *If . . .* has a connection to the famous Kipling poem of the same name, based on a script by David Sherwin and John Howlett called *Crusaders*. Lindsay uses the English public school system as a metaphor for the state of Britain then (and now), and the repression of the individual by society and authority. To this effect he employs a Brechtian device, mixing black and white footage with colour, on a quite arbitrary basis. (Though a more realistic reason for this may have been due to a lack of sufficient funds.)

As Anderson explained,

Appearing when it did, at the end of a year of youthful dissidence and revolt, If . . . has often seemed to be a film made purposely to reflect the revolutionary fervour of the Sixties. The truth is different. Seth Holt had offered me the script and I responded to the story because I approved of its romantic and rebellious spirit and because there was so much of my own experience that could relate directly to the subject and not just my experience as a schoolboy but my experience of society in the years that had followed.

Not since Vigo's *Zéro de Conduite*, an influence he acknowledges in the film's final sequence, has a director shown such a rapport with the mind and attitude of his young cast.

Lindsay is one of the very few directors who actually likes actors [said Malcolm McDowell]. For some he is patient and gentle. He can also be very firm. Somehow . . . he brings out the best in the people around him. He expects contributions and likes to work in the spirit of collaboration with his team . . . When he directs actors, there is never a feeling of being 'directed' since he generates an atmosphere where everyone can create.

Alan Lovell wrote, 'One thing to be said about Anderson's work immediately is that it is a great achievement simply to have got that work produced within the (British) cinema, work which isn't straightforwardly naturalistic but raises problems about conventions and so on.'

Shown in Cannes in 1968, the year of student revolt around the world, the film seemed cut out of the pavements of Paris, and won the Golden Palm.

DIRECTOR: Lindsay Anderson

SCREENPLAY: David Sherwin

PHOTOGRAPHY: Miroslav Ondricek

MUSIC: Marc Wilkinson; Sanctus 'Missa Lubba'

LEADING PLAYERS: Malcolm McDowell, David Wood, Richard Warwick, Robert Swann, Christine Noonan, Hugh Thomas, Rupert Webster, Peter Jeffrey, Anthony Nicholls, Arthur Lowe, Mona Washbourne

PRODUCTION COMPANY: Memorial Enterprises

COUNTRY: GB

DATE: 1968

Although one should be wary of stories about Fellini, especially those propagated by himself, he is quoted as saying that he would have become a circus performer if he had not discovered moving images, thanks to meeting Roberto Rossellini. He also apparently ran away from home to join a circus at the age of 12, in true storybook tradition. Circuses and fairgrounds certainly appear time and time again in his films, and, like Orson Welles, he is something of a magical performer.

Gelsomina (Fellini's wife and inspiration, Giulietta Masina) is the *mute* simple-minded peasant girl who becomes the devoted, mistreated assistant to Zampano (Anthony Quinn), the brutish itinerant circus strongman.

An enormous critical and sentimental success in Europe and America, where Masina's character was compared to Chaplin's 'Little Tramp' figure and to other silent clowns, and the film was hailed as a 'modern morality play', it won the New York critics and Best Foreign Language Oscar for 1956. In historian Arthur Knight's view, this 'intriguing mixture of poetry and realism' was also an early example of the value Nino Rota's music played in most of Fellini's films, with his four-theme score, the main motif played by a trumpet. The song, with and without lyrics, shared in the glory.

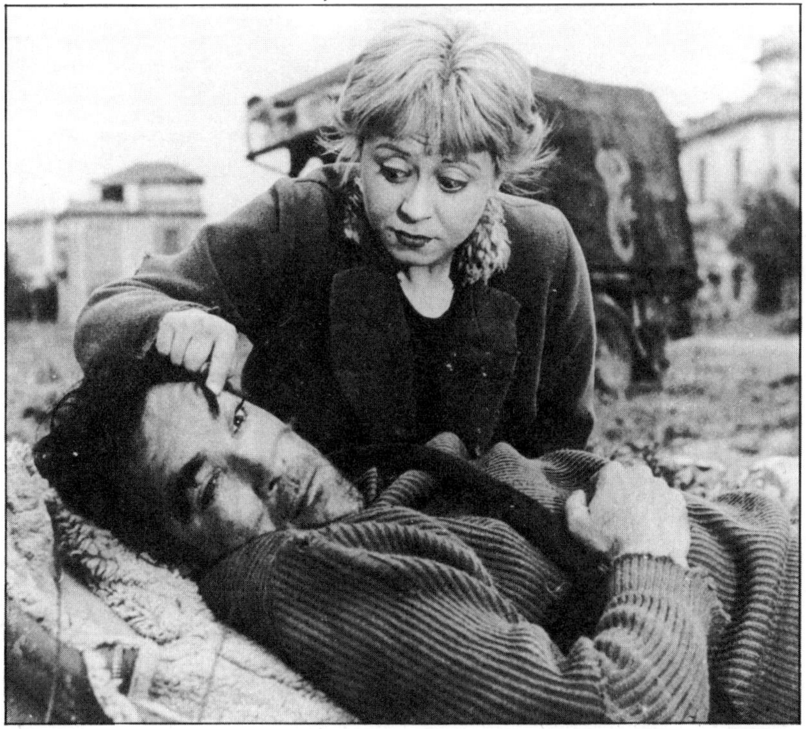

DIRECTOR: Federico Fellini

SCREENPLAY: Federico Fellini, Tullio Pinelli

PHOTOGRAPHY: Otello Martelli

MUSIC: Nino Rota

LEADING PLAYERS: Giulietta Masina, Anthony Quinn, Richard Basehart, Aldo Silvani, Marcella Rovere

PRODUCTION COMPANY: Ponti-de Laurentiis

COUNTRY: Italy

DATE: 1954

AI-NO CORRIDA

EMPIRE OF THE SENSES

Like so many of the British and French critics who turned director in the Fifties, the Japanese Nagisa Oshima went from writing about films to making them in 1959. But it was with his political and psycho-culturally explorative, sexually all-explicit film, *Ai-no corrida*, regarded at the time as the first film to break down the barriers between the commercial art film and hard-core pornography (*Last Tango* had gone some way towards this but with Marlon Brando in the lead, couldn't go quite as far as all that) that Oshima created a sensation at Cannes, where an unprecedented thirteen screenings were set up to meet demand. The jury, who were not swayed by the scenes of sex from Oshima's consistent treatment of sensitive issues, gave him the Best Director award. The film created storms around the world before going on to great success. Because of one scene using hard boiled eggs, the sale of eggs in the larger American cities increased dramatically.

The idea for the film (not the egg recipe) arose out of Oshima's French producer's request for a hard-core film. Shot entirely in Japan where the sight of a pubic hair in a developing lab brings down the police, the undeveloped film was processed in France and then re-imported to Japan with every strand air-brushed into a milky white haze. Oshima, whose film had been hailed as the first porno film for women, was arrested and prosecuted for the obscenity in his published screenplay. Four years later he was found innocent.

The true story, of a woman's all-consuming passion to possess her mate through sexual submission, occurred in 1936 on the eve of Japan's invasion of China. The woman, Sada, after numerous and increasingly more explicit sexual acts — saved from prurience (some feel) by much analytical talk and the admittance of others upon their games — which reach their climax when, because of their increasing need for violence to sustain sexual pleasure — 'My body is yours. Do as you like.' – she strangles her consenting lover – 'This time do not stop, it hurts too much afterwards.' Waking to find him dead she cuts off his genitalia, ties them up in her little red silken handkerchief and, clutching it close to her, roams the streets of Tokyo packed with soldiers and battle flags. Four days later, smiling contentedly, she is arrested, tried and jailed for murder. Sada became celebrated as a folk heroine. Her name, Oshima says, 'Is so popular in Japan, that to say it is enough to raise the question of the most serious sexual taboos.'

'It is true that I felt totally free to make this film as I wanted . . . To think of Sada as a murderess shocks me, as it would any Japanese. Sada and Kizhizo [the man] may seem to be libertines in the beginning but they move towards a form of sanctification and I hope everyone understands that.'

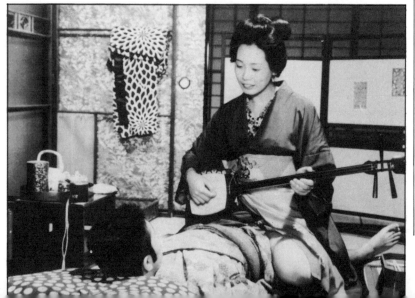

DIRECTOR:	Nagisa Oshima
SCREENPLAY:	Nagisa Oshima
PHOTOGRAPHY:	Hideo Ito
MUSIC:	Minoru Miki
LEADING PLAYERS:	Eiko Matsuda, Tatsuya Fuji, Aoi Nakajima, Taiji Tonoyama, Kanae Kobayashi, Melka Seri
PRODUCTION COMPANY:	Argos Films/Oshima
COUNTRY:	Japan/France
DATE:	1976

Columbia had originally bought the rights to C. S. Forester's *The African Queen* intending to make it with Charles Laughton and Elsa Lanchester. They sold it to Warner's who had Bette Davis and David Niven in mind for it but did nothing with it either. Huston was finishing work on *The Red Badge of Courage* and discussing *The African Queen* with independent producer Sam Spiegel, for his next project, but Warner's were asking $50,000. Spiegel went to Sound Services, a company that supplied equipment to the studios, for the money. John Huston recalled: 'Sound Services wasn't in the habit of making loans, but Sam was desperate, trying anything and everybody. . . . they agreed, gave Sam the money, and the rights to *The African Queen* were ours.'

The film, which marked the beginning of Huston's lengthy absence from the Hollywood studios, was shot on location on the Ruiki in the Belgian Congo, though certain scenes, all the ones with Humphrey Bogart and Katharine Hepburn in the water, had to be done in the studio in London. (The pollution thriving in the waters where they worked had been responsible for the lingering and debilitating illness that had ruined the life and career of lovely Edwina Booth when she made *Trader Horn* in Africa in 1929.) Robert Morley, who played the brother of Rose (Hepburn) in the beginning of the film, never left Pinewood studios, and the famous scene of Bogart pulling the *African Queen* through the leech-infested marshes was shot in a studio tank, though the leeches were real enough.

Huston and Bogart were celebrated boozers, and, in addition to drawing Bogart's 1951 Oscar winning performance out of him, Huston also shared Bogart's escape from an attack of malaria that decimated virtually everyone else on the crew. Jack Cardiff, the first cameraman, was laid low by malaria. The head sound man had to lie down before he fell down. It turned out that the bottled water had been polluted, and only Bogart and Huston escaped due to the enormous amounts of alcohol they were consuming. Other problems, according to Bogart, included an invasion by an army of soldier ants; labour troubles with the natives who went on strike every payday (pay being

DIRECTOR:	John Huston
SCREENPLAY:	James Agee, John Huston
PHOTOGRAPHY:	Jack Cardiff
MUSIC:	Allan Gray
LEADING PLAYERS:	Humphrey Bogart, Katharine Hepburn, Robert Morley, Peter Bull, Theodore Bikel
PRODUCTION COMPANY:	Romulus/Horizon
COUNTRY:	GB
DATE:	1952

rice, fish, cigarettes and 3s a day), and the non-arrival of the liquor supply upon which the entire cast (well, not Miss Hepburn, who didn't indulge, nor Huston and Bogart, who had their own private supply) threatened to quit.

Huston's work with Hepburn on the role of Rose, was a blend of broad strokes and intimate suggestions. He gave Eleanor Roosevelt's 'lovely little smile' as a guide to Hepburn's interpretation of the serious-minded, frustrated, missionary Rose.

Well, now Katie, you're going to go through this whole adventure before the falls and before love raises its . . . well, you know what I mean, solemn. Then I thought of how to remedy that. She's used to handling strangers as her brother's hostess. And you 'put on' a smile. Whatever the situation, like Mrs. Roosevelt – she felt she was ugly – she thought she looked better smiling – she she . . . chin up. The best is yet to come – onward ever onward. That society smile.

Hepburn smiled and the film was one of the top moneymakers of 1952.

It took more than sound and ten years of 'Talkies' – it took a war for Chaplin to at last make his first dialogue film. *The Great Dictator* was also the first time Chaplin worked with a complete script, a very long 300 pages, divided into 25 sections, each designated by a letter of the alphabet. The script was apparently completed on the day Britain declared war on Germany. Surprisingly, though he played two parts and spoke in both of them, dialogue also speeded up his shooting schedule, which, spread out across a formidable 168 days, was still way under his usual year-and-more-long schedules. Although Chaplin and Paulette Goddard, his leading lady from *Modern Times*, were in the process of getting divorced, he hired her for the role of the practical Hannah.

The film was a departure and a time of transition for him in other ways as well. Karl Struss joined Rollie Totheroh, Chaplin's cameraman for 23 years, as co-director of photography.

The shooting of Chaplin's two roles was done completely separately – first the role of the ghetto barber; then the dictator Hynkel scenes. Comedian Jack Oakie who had just been on a diet had to be fattened up for the role of Hynkel's rival dictator Napaloni.

Main shooting had been completed by March 1940, but the final speech was yet to be shot, the text of which took almost three months to write. This speech was used as text for his Christmas card by the director Archie Mayo, it was produced as a pamphlet by the Communist Party in England, and subsequently held against Chaplin during Hollywood's communist witch-hunts. It was as impassioned, sincerely felt and well wrought as any of his pantomime pieces.

Among the comedy set pieces are the encounter between Hynkel and Napaloni, the two dictators, who have to be courteous in public but whose rivalry, in private, culminates in the finest tradition of the Sennett Keystone slapstick comedies in a battle with dishes full of spaghetti during a state banquet; the earlier ballet of the barber shop chairs between the two; and the allegorical, absurd, yet on the other hand lyrical dance of dictator Hynkel with the great blow-up globe of the world, which explodes, and frightens Hynkel up the curtain. The barber scene one remembers is where the little barber shaves a client in strict time to Brahms' Hungarian Dance.

The film had its World Premiere in New York, 15 October 1940.

DIRECTOR:	Charles Chaplin
SCREENPLAY:	Charles Chaplin
PHOTOGRAPHY:	Karl Struss, Rollie Totheroh
LEADING PLAYERS:	Charles Chaplin, Paulette Goddard, Jack Oakie, Reginald Gardiner, Henry Daniell, Carter De Haven, Grace Hale
PRODUCTION COMPANY:	United Artists
COUNTRY:	USA
DATE:	1940

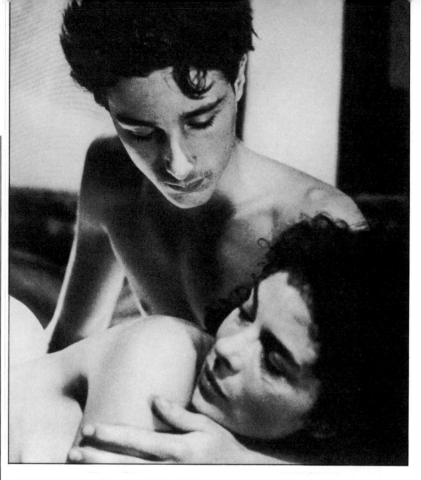

E dgar Reitz's film saga about life in a fictitious German village between 1919 and 1982, and centred around the figure of Maria (Marita Breuer), is one of the longest films ever made. Running for 15 hours and 40 minutes, in black and white and colour, it is 19 minutes longer than Fassbinder's monumental *Berlin-Alexanderplatz*, also originally made to be shown on TV.

The story, developed by Reitz between January and May 1979, took five years and four months from its inception to its release. It took a year, from June 1979 to July 1980 to write with Steinbach. Pre-production went from September 1980 to April 1981, and shooting lasted for 282 days, from May 1981 to November 1982. Editing finished in December 1983. The cast required 28 leading players, 140 speaking parts and 5,000 non-professionals.

We Germans have a hard time with our stories [explained Reitz]. It is our own history that stands in our way. The year 1945, the nation's 'zero hour' wiped out a lot, created a gap in people's ability to remember. As Mitschelich put it, an entire people had been made 'unable to mourn.' In our case that means, 'unable to tell stories' because our memories are obstructed by the great historical events they are connected with. Even now, after 40 years, we are still troubled by the weight of moral judgements, we are still afraid that our little, personal stories, could recall our Nazi past and remind us of our mass participation in the Third Reich.

Our film, Heimat, *consists of these suppressed or forgotten little stories . . . . Our film takes place in those human gardens called villages. We are taking a close look. We try to avoid making judgements.*

DIRECTOR: Edgar Reitz

SCREENPLAY: Edgar Reitz, Peter Steinbach

PHOTOGRAPHY: Gernot Roll

MUSIC: Nikos Mamangakis

LEADING PLAYERS: Willi Burger, Gertrud Bredel, Rudiger Weigang, Karin Rasenack, Dieter Schaad, Michael Lesch, Karin Kienzler, Gudrun Landgrebe, Jorge Richter, Marita Breuer, Jorge Hube, etc.

PRODUCTION COMPANY: Edgar Reitz Filmproduktion/WDR/SFB

COUNTRY: West Germany

DATE: 1984

O ne source for our film about T. E. Lawrence is his own book, The Seven Pillars of Wisdom. . . . The script is essentially [Robert] Bolt's conception of Lawrence. [Lawrence was Bolt's first script for the screen.] It is very close to my own conception of Lawrence, too . . . . Except for a very short prologue we have dealt in the film only with Lawrence's two years in the desert . . . . These two years were, in fact, Lawrence's whole life. Mostly I hope we have created a very exceptional hero.

DIRECTOR: David Lean

SCREENPLAY: Robert Bolt

PHOTOGRAPHY: F. A. Young

MUSIC: Maurice Jarre

LEADING PLAYERS: Peter O'Toole, Alec Guinness, Anthony Quinn, Jack Hawkins, Omar Sharif, Jose Ferrer, Anthony Quayle, Claude Rains, Arthur Kennedy

PRODUCTION COMPANY: Horizon Pictures

COUNTRY: GB

DATE: 1962

Thus David Lean for an interview he gave *Films and Filming* about the making of his film. It re-united him with producer Sam Spiegel (with whom he had made *The Bridge on the River Kwai*), and remains the most honoured and popular of his films in a long career that began as an editor (he supervised the editing himself, particularly the tricky action sequences), becoming a director in 1942 with *In Which We Serve*, and, though sporadic, has remained active.

Much of the film was shot in Jordan, where many of Lawrence's exploits took place. The technicians found remnants of the Turkish railroad that Lawrence and his Arabs dynamited forty years earlier – the metal lying unrusted in the sun. (Two trains had to be blown up for the film.)

Lawrence starts quietly, T. E. Lawrence talking to his fellow officers recalling his days in the desert. Suddenly, it cuts from the match that lights the cigarette, to one of the most spectacular views in the history of the cinema, or so it certainly felt to a public who were thus transported from the dark cramped intimate atmosphere of a room to what seemed no less than all the deserts of Arabia under the jewelled gaze of an all encompassing sun. 'Lawrence was bitten by the desert and by the people of the desert . . . and there is nothing like this big screen process for showing it.'

Lean's achievement, one among many, was that after such a start and such a location he never allowed the characters to dwindle or the intimate story to lose its grasp.

The film, which runs for more than three and a half hours, concerns itself with the 'legendary' British officer's mystical involvement with the Arabs, their cause, and the powerful attraction of the desert and its people on the English subconscious. Marlon Brando was unavailable for the role, and Alec Guinness (who had just played a Lawrence-like character on the stage, in *Ross*), was too old for the film (he played Prince Feisal) so Peter O'Toole, a 27-year-old Shakespearian actor with little previous film experience was cast as the 28-year-old Lawrence. Lean surrounded O'Toole with the finest British and American stage and screen stars of their generation.

The late Alex Korda once told me: 'If you get a good story with a good situation and two good characters you are half way home. If you get three good characters, you are very lucky. If you get four you can go down on your knees.' And we have more than four.

It was voted the Academy Award for Best Film of 1962.

SIGNS OF LIFE

LEBENSZEICHEN

Made in 1968, this was the German director Werner Herzog's first feature-length film. It was shot on Crete and the Island of Kos (where Herzog's grandfather had spent many years as an archaeologist), and is based on Achim von Arnim's early-nineteenth-century story *The Mad Invalid of Fort Ratonneau*. The film portrays the 'madness' that befalls a German soldier called Stroszek (not to be confused with the film and character of the same name which Herzog made nine years later, in 1977), who, along with his Greek wife and two other soldiers, is sent in 1942, during the height of the war, to convalesce on an island that lies outside the combat zone.

Fine black and white photography convey the hot summer weather, the remoteness and the man's gradual descent into madness.

Stroszek is another of those intense (Herzog-like) figures which were to be found in his later films, where they were usually embodied by the actor Klaus Kinski, but here played by Peter Brogle.

Much concerned with myths and folklore, Herzog also has a distrust of chickens, and for a scene in *Signs of Life*, one of the soldiers hypnotizes the farmyard fowl.

DIRECTOR: Werner Herzog

SCREENPLAY: Werner Herzog

PHOTOGRAPHY: Thomas Mauch

MUSIC: Stavros Xarchakos

LEADING PLAYERS: Peter Brogle, Wolfgang Reichmann, Julio Pinheiro, Athina Zacharopoulou, Wolfgang von Ungern-Sternberg, Wolfgang Stumpf, Henry van Lyck, Florian Fricke, Dr. Heinz Usener, Achmed Hafiz

PRODUCTION COMPANY: Werner Herzog Filmproduktion

COUNTRY: West Germany

DATE: 1968

That is the question set by Shakespeare and resolved by Lubitsch in this awesome, mordantly funny, timeless comedy about man's ability to survive even the most horrifying situations by remaining true to his own wonderful little self. During this century's most horrendous confrontations with its darkest nature, Lubitsch, the master of the light touch, created this work in which tears are wrung from the absurdity, and laughter from the horror.

Lubitsch's involvement with the tragedy being perpetuated by his native land must have been as great as that of any in America at the time, not merely because he was also Jewish, but because he had begun his brilliant career in Germany. Many of the people still living and working there were friends: so deep was his grief and revulsion over the events leading up to the war that he cancelled his plans in 1937 to film *Der Rosenkavalier* because the opera's composer, Richard Strauss, though not a sympathizer, had failed to use his enormous prestige to stand up against the rise of anti-semitism, even when it affected Strauss's long-time collaborator Hugo von Hoffmanstahl.

All of life is a comedy and Lubitsch set his in conquered Poland and focused it around a group of self-obsessed actors and how they dealt with their Nazi nemesis. Instead of the typical propaganda works of that time which souped up the usual wailing widows, innocents cowering in bunkers and prison camps, bone-crunching villains and mythological acts of self-sacrificing heroism to whip up a patriotic frenzy in the audience, Lubitsch side-stepped this 'honourable' task to see and show events with the clarity and genius normally associated only with hindsight.

'They name a brandy after Napoleon, a herring after Bismark, and Hitler is going to finish up as a piece of cheese,' one of the bit-part players observes to his colleague. Recognized since as the masterpiece it is, showing almost continuously in cinemas in Jerusalem, where the people who go to see it would have a far better appreciation of the film's bias, it was attacked at the time of its release as being in 'bad taste'. Lubitsch answered his critics:

DIRECTOR:	Ernst Lubitsch
SCREENPLAY:	Edwin Justus Mayer
PHOTOGRAPHY:	Rudolph Mate
MUSIC:	Werner Heymann
LEADING PLAYERS:	Carole Lombard, Jack Benny, Robert Stack, Felix Bressart, Lionel Atwill, Stanley Ridges, Sig Ruman, Tom Dugan, Charles Halton, George Lynn
PRODUCTION COMPANY:	Romaine Film/Alexander Korda
COUNTRY:	USA
DATE:	1942

When, in To Be or Not to Be, *I have referred to the destruction of Warsaw, I have shown it in all seriousness; the commentation under the shots of the devastated Warsaw speaks for itself and cannot leave any doubt in the spectator's mind what my voice and attitude towards these acts of horror is. What I have satirized in this picture are the Nazis and their ridiculous ideology. I have also satirized actors who remain actors however dangerous the situation might be, which I believe is a true observation.*

It is impossible to cite individual performances and contributions to this film since, once begun, an endless number of images, of detail in the performances, the script, the many parts that make up a film, would all deserve equal mention. Just writing and thinking about it again, everything in me wants to throw caution to the winds, proclaim this simply one of the greatest films ever made, and let the film take over.

In 1983 Mel Brooks made a technicolour remake starring himself and his wife, the actress Anne Bancroft. It was funny but *not* Lubitsch.

MEET ME IN ST LOUIS

Producer Arthur Freed stated that the film's timeless appeal 'was based on characters. The only story there was was "There's no place like home." This was especially true when home is deep-in-the-heart of America's mainland and the family is as warm, cosy, comfortable, attractive, charming, talented, loving, tuneful, and well-off as the Smith family of St Louis. (Mary Astor, who had already played a mistress (*The Great Lie*), a murderess (*Maltese Falcon*) now played the mother with the same consummate fearless skill that made type-casting inevitable.)

It was only Minnelli's third film.

Meet Me . . . was based on a series of original short stories written by Sally Benson which had appeared with great success in the New Yorker. *When Arthur Freed asked me what I thought of the idea of doing a film based on them I was very excited, because I could see them as people. From the first I wanted Judy Garland for it. At that time she was riding very high at MGM and was against doing it. Everyone was telling her that it would kill her career. She came to me full of objections. She had already been to see Arthur and hadn't got anywhere with him . . . but she thought she could make short shrift of me. When I finished explaining what I had in mind and how right she would be for the film, she left my office bewildered, having agreed to do it.*

As Esther Smith, the role turned out to be one of Garland's sweetest, least neurotic performances, and the first step away from the drab persona she had been stuck in up till that time. With this film and others in which she was directed by Minnelli, who would become her husband, Garland flowered on the screen. Besides a flawless cast, the film also benefited enormously from its score which included 'The Trolley Song', 'Have Yourself a Merry Little Christmas', 'The Boy Next Door', and the title song.

DIRECTOR: Vincente Minnelli

SCREENPLAY: Fred Finklehoffe, Irving Brecher

PHOTOGRAPHY: George Folsey

MUSIC: George Stoll

LEADING PLAYERS: Judy Garland, Margaret O'Brien, Mary Astor, Lucille Bremer, Leon Ames, Tom Drake, Marjorie Main, Harry Davenport, June Lockhart

PRODUCTION COMPANY: MGM

COUNTRY: USA

DATE: 1944

Orson Welles had the idea of making a documentary reconstruction of the career of Landru, the early-nineteenth-century French wife-murderer, a sort of modern Bluebeard. (The subject, a fertile one for the cinema, had already been treated in an elegantly made small-budget 1944 period film called *Bluebeard* by Edgar Ulmer, and would subsequently serve Claude Chabrol for his 1962 film about Landru.) Welles wanted Chaplin to play one of the principal roles. Instead Chaplin told Welles that it had given him the idea for a comedy, with himself in the principal role, the first time in almost forty years in which Chaplin would not be essaying the character of the Tramp. He paid Welles $5,000 for his original suggestion and the option (which Welles took up) to add a screen credit, 'Idea suggested by Orson Welles'.

In many ways, this film was a return in style to Chaplin's classic sophisticated silent comedy *A Woman of Paris*, except that, where that film had concerned a woman of many lovers, *Verdoux*, truly a black comedy, would be about a man with many wives. Edna Purviance, Chaplin's earliest, longest and best leading lady, who had played the central character in the silent film, was tested for the role of Madame Grosnay – it was the first time Chaplin and Edna had met for over twenty years, though she was not in the film.

With the release of *Monsieur Verdoux*, with its pacifistic line, a smear campaign was launched against Chaplin, headed by the American Legion. It was the dawn of the McCarthy era, and Chaplin was subpoenaed by the House un-American Activities Committee to testify on his alleged Communist affiliations. Chaplin wired back, 'I am not a Communist; neither have I ever joined any political party or organization in my life. I am what you call a peace-monger.' Pressure groups organized boycotts against the film and successfully restricted its circulation after its premiere on 11 April 1947. Though it was not a great success with the public, who were less troubled by his politics than by the thought of their beloved and much-married 'Charlie' as a multiple wife-murderer, it was nevertheless voted the Best Film of the year by the National Board of Review, and is considered by some of his critics and admirers to be his best work.

DIRECTOR: Charles Chaplin

SCREENPLAY: Charles Chaplin

PHOTOGRAPHY: Rollie Totheroh, Curt Courant, Wallace Chewing

MUSIC: Charles Chaplin

LEADING PLAYERS: Charles Chaplin, Martha Raye, Isobel Elsom, Marilyn Nash, Robert Lewis, Mady Correll, Allison Rodell

PRODUCTION COMPANY: Chaplin/United Artists

COUNTRY: USA

DATE: 1947

BRIEF ENCOUNTER

A sk an Englishman about the 1940s, and the movies he remembers, and he will begin with *Brief Encounter*. It was David Lean's third film, and his third and last from a story by Noël Coward. Coward, having amused theatre audiences for years with his urbane witticisms, turned in 1945 to the screen adaptation of his one-act play, *Still Life*.

In many ways it has the structure of the typical unhappy screen romances. A young married woman has a chance meeting with a young doctor on a railway station. They fall in love at first sight, have a tortuous unconsummated affair, and finally give each other up.

In the closing sequence, as Alec (Trevor Howard) is leaving Laura (Celia Johnson) for the last time, we see his hand linger on her cloth-coated shoulder for a moment. When he has left she rushes out to the rail platform to throw herself on to the tracks as the express train comes screeching through. But suicide is not in her nature, any more than infidelity, and the lights of the train pound her tortured face in rhythm with the clattering wheels. Back in the station diner her friend's conversation overwhelms her, just as the grotesque close-up of her friend's mouth overwhelms us.

Ronald Neame who co-produced recalled that casting the two leads was essential to the delicate balance Coward was trying to achieve: 'Noël was a stickler for casting correctly as opposed to casting for names. He was determined we should have Celia Johnson.' David Lean recalled:

I first saw Trevor in a rough cut of a reel from The Way to the Stars. *He had one shot on an aerodrome – and I'll never forget it. A plane came in over the field and did a victory roll. Trevor looked up and said, 'Lineshoot'. It was wonderful. Just that one word, the way he said it and the way he looked. I said, 'That's him' and went to Noël.*

I still have an affection for Brief Encounter. *I have never really got over it. We were making* Great Expectations *when it came out and I had the first print during our location work on the Romney marshes. We got it down to the local cinema and screened it as a sneak preview. It started; and during the first love scene a woman in the front row started laughing, a terrible cackling chicken's laugh. Then everyone else in the cinema started to laugh. And every love scene that came up, this woman started to laugh and the whole cinema was rolling in the aisles. I went back in the evening wondering how I could get into Denham Laboratories and burn the negative. I was so terribly ashamed of my work. So every time anyone mentions* Brief Encounter *I think, 'Oh yes, very nice in the art houses but what the hell happened out of town.' A lesson in humility may be food for everyone; but I didn't need a lesson in humility in those days. I was a very frightened young man.*

DIRECTOR:	David Lean
SCREENPLAY:	Noël Coward, David Lean, Anthony Havelock Allan
PHOTOGRAPHY:	Robert Krasker
MUSIC:	Rachmaninov's Second Piano Concerto
LEADING PLAYERS:	Celia Johnson, Trevor Howard, Stanley Holloway, Joyce Carey, Cyril Raymond, Everley Gregg
PRODUCTION COMPANY:	Cineguild
COUNTRY:	Great Britain
DATE:	1945

Together, director Anthony Mann and actor James Stewart made eight movies between *Winchester 73* (which had originally been assigned to Fritz Lang) in 1950 and *The Man from Laramie* in 1955. *The Far Country* was the fourth of their five Westerns together and established Stewart as one of the leading Western stars. Stewart, who made his personal fortune with these films, was a willing worker, learning how to handle a rifle for *Winchester 73*, and fight under horses' hoofs.

As so often in their films, he was the man with the painful past. But Mann used Stewart's already established charming, bemused side, to make his character's cynicism palatable, and he softened the often violent edges of the story. The film also marked Mann's last collaboration with scriptwriter Borden Chase (*Winchester 73* and *Bend of the River*), a specialist in quality Westerns and action pictures like *Red River*, *Vera Cruz* and *Man Without a Star*, often adapted from his own stories.

Mann was a meticulous craftsman with a keen eye for spectacular outdoor cinematography and an instinctive sense for the visual expression of inner conflicts. In an interview he gave to *Films and Filming* in 1964, he explained his predelection for Westerns: 'Why is the American Western film such a success throughout the world? It is because a man says, "I'm going to do something." – And does it: We all want to be heroes. This is what drama is. This is what pictures are all about. I don't believe in anything else.'

DIRECTOR: Anthony Mann

SCREENPLAY: Borden Chase

PHOTOGRAPHY: William Daniels

MUSIC: Joseph Gershenon

LEADING PLAYERS: James Stewart, Ruth Roman, Corinne Calvert, Walter Brennan, John McIntire, Jay C. Flippen, Henry Morgan, Steve Brodie, Royal Dano, Jack Elam

PRODUCTION COMPANY: Universal-International

COUNTRY: USA

DATE: 1955

FREEKS

Olga Baclanova, who played the treacherous Queen of the Air, recalled director Tod Browning's admonition before he introduced her to her co-workers, "'Now I show you with whom you are going to play. But don't faint." I say, "Why should I faint?" He takes me and shows me all the freaks there. . . . At first I wanted to faint. I wanted to cry when I saw them. They have such nice faces but it is so terrible. . . . Now, after we start that picture, I like them all so much.'

Tod Browning, famed for his silent horror films with Lon Chaney and the first *Dracula*, was not a director known for his style as much as for his subject matter. With the exception of *Freaks*, he dealt with monsters created for the screen without ever creating an uproar. Somehow the powers that be at MGM, who could not have foreseen the result, gave him the go-ahead to make this film about real people, nature's unfortunates, Randian, the Hindu Living Torso, Josephine-Joseph, the half-man half-woman, Martha, the armless wonder, the Hilton Siamese twins as well as assorted pinheads, midgets and the usual circus sideshow people.

The story revolved around the circus strong man and the glamorous trapeze artist plotting to rob the midget of his money, by taking advantage of the small man's love for her, to marry and then to kill him. The film contained a series of unforgettable sequences, such as the wedding party with all the freaks in attendance. But most shocking of all was the freaks' revenge on the treacherous duo, killing him and turning her into a human chicken. Because these were not movie-created monsters but real-people playing characters like themselves, the shock and rejection by studio and audiences were all the greater.

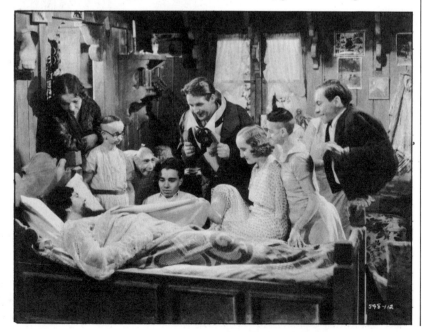

598-12

The preview running time was 90 minutes, but it was recut immediately after. It was banned in Britain and after its initial failure Metro tried to re-issue it under the title *Nature's Freaks* and some awful publicity: 'What's the sex of an androgyne? Are the Siamese Twins in love?' And a prologue indicating that history had thrown up a number of famous freaks, including Kaiser Wilhelm II! Nothing worked. It was then put under wraps for more than twenty years.

In 1962 a re-edited version, at a running time of 64 minutes, was released with another prologue and shown at the Cannes Film Festival. It has become a cult classic.

DIRECTOR:	Tod Browning
SCREENPLAY:	Willis Goldbeck, Leon Gordon
PHOTOGRAPHY:	Merrit B. Gerstad
LEADING PLAYERS:	Wallace Ford, Olga Baclanova, Leila Hyams, Roscoe Ates
PRODUCTION COMPANY:	MGM
COUNTRY:	USA
DATE:	1932

Curiously, Fritz Lang – one of the screen's legendary and most innovative directors, the creator of *Metropolis*, *M* and *Fury* – is represented in the Top 100 by this untypical and unlikely 1955 swashbuckling costume melodrama which was presented to him as an assignment by MGM, with script already written. It was Lang's only film in Cinemascope, a process he would describe in Godard's film, *Le Mepris*, as being 'not for men, but for snakes and funerals'. Subsequently Lang disowned the film – saying that it was re-edited by MGM after his work was completed: he had omitted the happy ending provided in the script based on the novel of the same name by John Meade Falkner, and was angry when he found that it had been added to the film after he had finished work on it. However, he reserved the right to change his mind and as the film rose in critical esteem he professed to be happier with what was actually a rather ambiguous ending.

This gothic story, set along the storm-swept Cornish coast, was shot in 45 days on locations in Oceanside, California and possessed all the trappings we associate with such things – a churchyard, wind, owls hooting at night, thunderstorms, mystery houses, and a rich, almost Dickensian atmosphere throughout with which Lang shrouded the story and enthralled and mystified the viewer. Indeed, *Moonfleet* is almost a classic example of a consummate artist spinning gold out of a sow's ear, for with his expertise and a superb crew of technicians – the music, costumes, superior art direction and rich photography to assist his design – this hokum attained delirious heights. Interestingly, the only other Lang film almost to make this list was his next film, *While the City Sleeps*, a crime in the city/newspaper melodrama with an all-B or fading-star cast that looked and sounded even better when it was translated into German, the country to which he would return, and where he made his last films, after what he had felt to have been twenty years of endless clashes with the American studios and his disgust over the mutilation of his films by them.

DIRECTOR: Fritz Lang

SCREENPLAY: Margaret Fitts

PHOTOGRAPHY: Robert Planck

MUSIC: Miklos Rozsa

LEADING PLAYERS: Stewart Granger, John Whitely, George Sanders, Joan Greenwood, Viveca Lindfors

PRODUCTION COMPANY: MGM

COUNTRY: USA

DATE: 1955

THE NIGHT OF THE LIVING DEAD

THE NIGHT OF THE FLESH EATERS

The difference here, and with earlier stories revelling in the undead, was the fact that this was the night the zombies won. Just when you thought it was safe to go to your grave, they were there in the graveyard to greet you and eat you. The film was filmed locally in Pittsburgh, where Romero lived. He obtained local funding and cast his friends in the movie. 'Most of the people were actually from the small town we shot in,' he said. 'We had quite a bit of co-operation from people here in the city – the police and city fathers . . . happy to have guns in their hands.'

By making it totally explicit, unlike the atmospheric and intellectual Val Lewton variations on such themes – i.e. *I Walked with a Zombie* – Romero's, unlike Lewton's living dead, had more life in them, and, what an appetite! One of the films alternative titles far more aptly described the plot in *The Night of the Flesh Eaters*. By turning life after death into one long movable feast, Romero brought horror back into horror films, though too much for the

average 1960s neighbourhood movie houses which refused to show it, driving it to the drive-ins and a young audience hungry for something fresh. It became a cult classic, as is so often the way with things forbidden or rejected by the establishment.

Eschewing the glossy look of colour film (for which he was offered a budget) Romero chose instead the flat, murky ambiance of black and white to portray the American-Gothic landscape in which the film occurs. It is an intense, well-structured 96 minutes, unrelieved by any of the conventional horror film distractions of comedy, romance, or explanatory old gents. The lovers, two characters perhaps expected to survive a film like this, are roasted alive in their car and devoured before the film is half over. At the climax, the WASP father discovers that his daughter, risen from the dead down in the cellar, is busily devouring her own mother. And all we are told about these zombies is by a TV newsreader who says: 'The ghouls are ordinary people . . . but in a kind of trance.'

And of course, there was the touch that brought the critics to write excitedly of the film's complex socio/psychological/political ideas – the main character is a black man, a fact which is never once mentioned in the film, and he still dies in the end, shot by the white rescuers who mistake him for one of the culprits. At least the zombies, unlike the living, do not suffer from prejudice. They eat anything.

To an older generation the film had no character development, little plot and, worst of all, a total lack of taste. To their sons and daughters, growing up, like the director, on a literary diet of horror comics this was neither a problem nor the case. The film's influence was soon apparent in the wave of zombie-like movies and movies about zombies that followed. While the next generation of filmmakers would take the genre to a more sophisticated level, i.e. John Carpenter's *Halloween*, Wes Craven's *Nightmare on Elm Street*, Romero happily and profitably continued to mine the same vein with films like *The Crazies, Martin, Zombies, Creepshow* and *Dawn of the Dead* without ever stretching credulity.

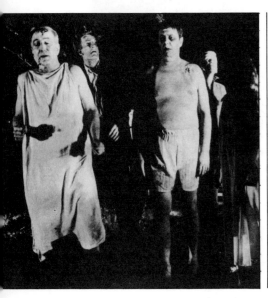

DIRECTOR: George A. Romero

SCREENPLAY: John A. Russo

PHOTOGRAPHY: George A. Romero

LEADING PLAYERS: Judith O'Dea, Duane Jones, Karl Hardman, Keith Wayne, Judith Ridley, Marilyn Eastman, Russell Streiner, Kyra Schon

PRODUCTION COMPANY: Image Ten

COUNTRY: USA

DATE: 1969

Hitchcock hadn't made a black and white film for a long time when he made *Psycho*, in black and white, as if he didn't take the project seriously, rather more like a doodle along the edge of his more important work. Originally he had planned to make it for his TV series. The film lacked what could be called a 'star' cast except in the loosest sense. It was a departure from his smoothly crafted, all-star-casting, middle-aged, middle-of-the-road audience thrillers. With *Psycho* he aimed (with cynical disregard) at a youthful public, the one who only went to very few films anymore, who had, in fact rejected almost all the movies being made in Hollywood by the major distributors. And he caught them. The old master had made his youngest film. Its phenomenal box-office success turned it into a social phenomenon.

During the shower scene I leapt out of my seat and bit my thumb half off in terror. Just sheer bloody terror. The warm water. Her mouth wide open. The plastic shower curtain. The knife. The water – turning red at her feet. I'm not sure I saw it all, clearly, beyond that first slash. I'd never been that frightened before in a movie and I haven't been that frightened in one since.

Anyone who grew up in the years since Janet Leigh was killed by Norman Bates – isn't it strange how everyone remembers the name of Tony Perkins' clean-cut all-American psycho but Janet Leigh's Marion will always be remembered as Janet Leigh – in that horrible motel murder will have seen innumerable films with even worse cases to shock them. Yet, even without the 'surprise' *Psycho* remains a classic example of the school Hitchcock was master of. For *Psycho* is pure film. Its hold is based on the fundamental reason for movies' enormous appeal, our voyeurism. And no director ever played on the more prurient aspect of our fascination with our and our fellows' navels with quite the same diabolical skill and astuteness.

The gothic house on the hill behind the motel, where Norman Bates lived with his 'mother', is now a landmarked building on the lot of Universal studios. To date, there have been two sequels, with Anthony Perkins repeating his original role.

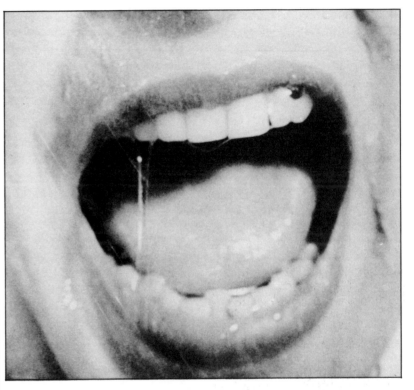

DIRECTOR: Alfred Hitchcock

SCREENPLAY: Joseph Stefano

PHOTOGRAPHY: John L. Russell

MUSIC: Bernard Herrmann

LEADING PLAYERS: Anthony Perkins, Janet Leigh, John Gavin, Vera Miles, John McIntyre, Martin Balsam, Simon Oakland

PRODUCTION COMPANY: Shamley

COUNTRY: USA

DATE: 1960

Hitchcock had read Daphne du Maurier's *Rebecca* while the book was still in galleys and had made an offer to buy the rights, but her agent's asking price was too high and Hitchcock had to pass. David Selznick didn't have the same financial constraints, however, and began negotiating with Hitchcock to direct the film even before the actual purchase had been made. A telegram he sent to Hitchcock describes the casting possibilities that he was considering for the Laurence Olivier role:

Regret to inform you Ronald Colman so fearful about murder angle and also about possibility of picture emerging as woman-starring vehicle that he will not do it unless he sees treatment . . . can sign Leslie Howard for it . . . Bill Powell has been absolutely wild about role and anxious to do it but I turned him down on expectation of Ronald Colman.

Selznick wanted the story of the book followed very closely, just as he had with *Gone with the Wind*. He had a theory that people who had read the book would be upset if they saw something different on the screen, and so Michael

DIRECTOR: Alfred Hitchcock

SCREENPLAY: Robert E. Sherwood, Joan Harrison

PHOTOGRAPHY: George Barnes

MUSIC: Franz Waxman

LEADING PLAYERS: Laurence Olivier, Joan Fontaine, George Sanders, Judith Anderson, Nigel Bruce, Reginald Denny, C. Aubrey Smith, Gladys Cooper

PRODUCTION COMPANY: Selznick/United Artists

COUNTRY: USA

DATE: 1940

Hogan's screenplay, and the rewrites by Joan Harrison and Robert E. Sherwood, managed to stick very closely to du Maurier's version. Max, for instance, was not allowed to shoot his first wife and get away with it, so her death was made accidental. Hitchcock later disowned the structure: 'It's not a Hitchcock picture, it's a novelette really. The story is old-fashioned, there was a period when this school of feminine literature was in fashion, and though I'm not against it, the fact is that the story is lacking in humour.'

The production, which began filming just as the Second World War broke out, was torn by competing personalities on and off the set. Hitchcock had a very personal creative style, one for which he was already world-famous, and Selznick belonged to the old school of Hollywood producers who wanted their movies to stick to the schedule, the script, and the producer's wishes. More than ever, he was determined to assert himself with Hitchcock, whose first American film this was. Joan Fontaine, 21 during the filming, recalls that Hitchcock deliberately created problems on the set:

To be honest, Hitchcock was divisive with us. He wanted total control over me, and he seemed to relish the cast not liking one another, actor for actor, by the end of the film. Now of course this helped my performance, since I was supposed to be terrified of everyone and it gave a lot of tension to my scenes. It kept him in command and it was upheaval he wanted.

Hitchcock later pointed out many flaws in the film, mainly in the narrative structure. Others too have pointed out that the film is too long (at 130 minutes it is one of his longest), and that the scenes away from Manderley dilute the power of the narrative. The story itself was not in the classic Hitchcock tradition, and the suspense that is built up around the characters' personality conflicts was introduced by Hitchcock himself.

But for all these reservations, audiences and critics loved the film at its release, and it went on to win the Oscar for Best Film. Joan Fontaine won her Oscar, often believed to have been due for her role in *Rebecca*, the following year, for her role in her next Hitchcock film, *Suspicion*.

VOYAGE TO ITALY/THE DIVORCEE OF NAPLES/THE GREATEST LOVE/
LOVE IS THE STRONGEST/THE LONELY WIFE(UK)

'I consider,' Rossellini once said, '*Viaggio* to be very important in my work. It was a film which rested on something very subtle, the variations in a couple's relationship under the influence of the third person; the exterior world surrounding them.'

Originally, his plan had been to adapt Colette's novel *Due*, but by the time his leading man, George Sanders, had arrived, he discovered that the rights had already been sold.

George Sanders, most of whose career had been spent in the Hollywood studios playing cynical cads with great nonchalant aplomb, found Rossellini's working methods excruciating. One day, this most sophisticated of actors was driven to tears and told his co-star, Ingrid Bergman, 'I can't go on. I can't do this comedia delle arte, and invent and get the line at the last moment.'

Ingrid herself, though Rossellini's wife and partner in five films, was doubtful about this, their third film together, and admitted in her autobiography: 'I was quite bewildered too, but I thought, Roberto is Roberto; he might do another magnificent *Open City*. After all, we're going to Naples, and he'll be inspired there.'

Sanders said, 'When I complained about the lack of a finished script, Rossellini decreed that I was an impossible man. People talk about neorealism . . . it's a joke. The real reason that Rossellini films in the streets is that studio sets cost money. I've seen some misers before, but I've never met anyone who could equal him. . . .'

In its total disregard of the laws of dramatic construction – nothing apparently happens, as there is virtually no action, and everything comes from within the characters who only provide a slender link for the audience to hold on to – this film was in some ways the purest form of cinema. Ahead of its time, it needed selling and consequently was given various titles on release (see above).

The film is a supreme example of the power of the close-up in its ability to convey the interior experience through exterior design, whether that of a beautiful face or a landscape. As such it was also a forerunner of Rossellini's former script-collaborator Antonioni's *L'Avventura*-like movies. Misunderstood, derided and rejected at the time, Rossellini's Bergman films today belong with his most remarkable work.

DIRECTOR:	Roberto Rossellini
SCREENPLAY:	Vitaliano Brancati, Rossellini
PHOTOGRAPHY:	Enzo Serafin
MUSIC:	Renzo Rossellini
LEADING PLAYERS:	Ingrid Bergman, George Sanders, Maria Mauban, Paul Muller
PRODUCTION COMPANY:	Italiafilm/Junior/Sveva/ Ariane/Francinex/SGC
COUNTRY:	Italy/France
DATE:	1953

THE
CRITICS' CHOICE

JOHN KOBAL
BORN: 1942

John Kobal, a Canadian, has written about films for numerous magazines and is the author of several books on the cinema since 1966. He also founded a photographic archive of film stills from Hollywood and has organized exhibitions over the past ten years to bring the art of the Hollywood portrait photographers into the limelight. His list is in alphabetical order.

All About Eve	Ivan the Terrible Parts I and II/ Ivan Groznyi*
Bel Ami	
Les Enfants du Paradis/ Children of Paradise*	Meet Me in St Louis*
	Morocco
Gilda	The Thief of Bagdad*
Gone with the Wind*	To Be or Not to Be*

FIRST MOVIE: *The Black Swan*.
FIRST FILM WALKED OUT OF/LEAST FAVOURITE MOVIE: *Romeo and Juliet* (Zeffirelli)
– I've been walking out of his films ever since.

An asterisk* denotes a film included in the top 100

JAN AGHED
BORN: 1934

Jan Aghed is a Swedish film critic and writes for the Malmö morning paper *Sydsvenska Daqbladet*, as well as for film journals. He occasionally speaks on radio and lectures on films. His list is in no particular order.

	The Seven Samurai/ Shichinin No Samurai*
	My Darling Clementine*
	The Quiet Man
	The Childhood of Maxim Gorky
	Les Enfants du Paradis/ Children of Paradise*
	Singin' in the Rain*
	The Band Wagon*
	Amarcord*
	Smiles of a Summer Night
	Some Like It Hot*

NESTOR ALMENDROS
BORN 1930

Nestor Almendros, one of the world's most distinguished cameramen, has written for various Cuban papers and magazines including *Revolución* and *Bohemia*, as well as for international film journals. He has published one book, *A Man with a Camera*.

1	Citizen Kane*
2	Les Quatre Cents Coups/ The 400 Blows
3	Aleksandr Nevskii/ Alexander Nevsky*
4	Design for Living
5	The Crowd
6	Madam De …/ The Earrings of Madame De …/ Diamond Earrings*
7	The Devil is a Woman
8	Lieutenant Sansho
9	Rebecca*
10	Le Notti de Cabiria/Cabiria/ Nights of Cabiria*

FIRST MOVIE: *Lost Horizon* (Capra)
FIRST FILM WALKED OUT OF/
LEAST FAVOURITE MOVIE: A film so insignificant that I don't even remember. Usually I stay to the end, even today.

LINDSAY ANDERSON
BORN: 1923

Lindsay Anderson is a British film and theatre director and critic. His films include *This Sporting Life* (1963), *If . . .* (1968), *O Lucky Man* (1972), *Britannia Hospital* (1982) and, most recently, *The Whales of August*.

1	L'Age D'Or/The Golden Age*
2	A Diary for Timothy
3	Earth/Zemlya*
4	A Generation
5	If . . .*
6	The Maltese Falcon*
7	Meet Me in St Louis*
8	They Were Expendable
9	Tokyo Story/ Tokyo Monogatari*
10	Zéro de Conduite/ Zero for Conduct*

FIRST MOVIE: *Chang* (Cooper and Shoedsack)

MARKE ANDREWS
BORN: 1950

Marke Andrews is film critic for the *Vancouver Sun*.

1	Citizen Kane*
2	Zéro de Conduite/ Zero for Conduct*
3	Badlands
4	Rashomon*
5	Midnight Cowboy
6	Psycho*
7	Slaughterhouse Five
8	Modern Times*
9	This Is Spinal Tap
10	One Flew Over The Cuckoo's Nest*

FIRST MOVIE: *All Quiet on the Western Front* (Milestone)
FIRST FILM WALKED OUT OF/
LEAST FAVOURITE MOVIE: *Howard the Duck*, not only because it's bad, but because it represents everything bad about the industry – wasteful budgets; stupid special effects; pandering to a 10-year-old's mentality.

NIGEL ANDREWS
BORN: 1947

Nigel Andrews has been the film critic for the *Financial Times* (London) since 1973. A regular broadcaster on BBC Radio, he has contributed to various cinema books and journals including *The Book of the Cinema* and *Sight and Sound*, and is the author of *Horror Films*.

1	Mirror/Zerkalo*
2	Heaven's Gate
3	Vertigo*
4	Citizen Kane*
5	Aguirre, Wrath of God
6	The Deer Hunter
7	La Passion de Jeanne d'Arc/ The Passion of Joan of Arc*
8	The Nutty Professor
9	Don't Look Now
10	Bring Me the Head of Alfredo Garcia

FIRST MOVIE: *Invaders from Mars* (Menzies)
FIRST FILM WALKED OUT OF: *Invaders from Mars* (in terror, but I was only six; I went back to see it later).
LEAST FAVOURITE MOVIE: Anything by Theo Angelopoulos (after *The Travelling Players*).

RICHARD BARKLEY
BORN: 1935

Richard Barkley has been film critic of the *Sunday Express* (London) since 1969. He began writing for a local Kent paper in 1962 under the compulsory pseudonym 'Cinecus', which inspired those who disagreed with him to call him 'Sillycus'.

1	The Seven Samurai/ Shichinin No Samurai*
2	Casablanca*
3	Fanny and Alexander/ Fanny och Alexander*
4	Heimat*
5	Battle of Algiers
6	Le Million
7	Shane
8	Zelig
9	Days and Nights in the Forest
10	Deliverance

FIRST MOVIE: *The Gold Rush* (Chaplin)
FIRST FILM WALKED OUT OF/
LEAST FAVOURITE MOVIE: *Husbands* (Cassavetes)
COMMENT: I recall seeing Chaplin's shorts projected at the wrong speed, or, as far as I was concerned then, the *right* speed. It seemed sorcery that one could be transfixed in mind and emotion by flickering images on a screen . . . My ten favourites are chosen because they conjure up for me hope, to appreciate them all over again without any sense of disappointment. There are other films which had such a profound effect on me I do not wish to risk diminishing their memory by a second look.

ROBERT BENAYOUN
BORN: 1926

Robert Benayoun is a French film critic, writer and director.

1	East of Eden*
2	La Règle du Jeu/ The Rules of the Game*
3	City Lights*
4	Citizen Kane*
5	L'Année Dernière à Marienbad/ Last Year at Marienbad*
6	Amarcord*
7	Viridiana*
8	L'Avventura*
9	Andrei Rublev*
10	The Maltese Falcon*

FIRST MOVIE: *Romeo and Juliet* (Cukor)
FIRST FILM WALKED OUT OF/
LEAST FAVOURITE MOVIE: *Breathless* (Godard)
COMMENT: Drawing this list, I always considered intrinsic sublimity, personal statement, achievement within work, intensity, magnetic hold, total subjectivity.

IRENE BIGNARDI
BORN: 1943

Irene Bignardi is literature and cinema correspondent for *La Repubblica* (Rome) and film critic for *L'Espresso* weekly magazine. She has also been the Director of Myst-Fest, the International Film Festival of Mystery and Police Films.

1	8½/Otto e Mezzo*
2	Amarcord*
3	The Gold Rush*
4	City Lights*
5	Modern Times*
6	Nashville
7	The Passenger
8	Bladerunner
9	2001: A Space Odyssey*
10	Some Like It Hot*

FIRST MOVIE: *Scaramouche* (Ingram)
FIRST FILM WALKED OUT OF/
LEAST FAVOURITE MOVIE: *Dune* (Lynch)

GUGLIELMO BIRAGHI

BORN: 1927

Guglielmo Biraghi has been film critic for *Il Messaggero* (Rome) since 1954, Director of the Taormina Film Festival since 1971, and is Director of the Venice Film Festival.

1	The Gold Rush*
2	Bicycle Thieves/ The Bicycle Thief/ Ladri di Biciclette*
3	Der Blaue Engel/ The Blue Angel
4	Rashomon*
5	The Seventh Seal/ Det Sjunde Inseglet*
6	Roma, Città Aperta/ Rome, Open City*
7	Andrei Rublev*
8	El Angel Exterminador/ The Exterminating Angel*
9	Les Années Lumières/ Light Years Away
10	Picnic at Hanging Rock

FIRST MOVIE: *Becky Sharp* (Mamoulian)
FIRST FILM WALKED OUT OF/
LEAST FAVOURITE MOVIE: So many!

JEAN-PIERRE BROSSARD

BORN: 1945

Jean-Pierre Brossard is a film historian and film critic for several Swiss, French and German papers and cine magazines. He is the Secretary-General of the International Federation of Film Societies and Vice-President of the International Council for Cinema and Television at UNESCO, Paris.

1	Battleship Potemkin/ Bronenosets Potyomkin*
2	Citizen Kane*
3	Tokyo Story/Tokyo Monogatari*
4	Modern Times*
5	Wild Strawberries/ Smultronstället*
6	Ashes and Diamonds/ Popiól i Diament*
7	Roma, Città Aperta/ Rome, Open City*
8	Hiroshima Mon Amour*
9	Viridiana*
10	Les Quatre Cents Coups/ The 400 Blows

FIRST MOVIE: *Les Quatre Cents Coups* (Truffaut); *L'Avventura* (Antonioni).

FREDDY BUACHE

BORN: 1924

Freddy Buache is film critic for the Swiss paper *Le Matin Lausanne*. As a film historian he has published some twenty books.

1	Sunrise*
2	Circus
3	Die Büchse der Pandora/ Pandora's Box
4	Bronenosets Potyomkin/ Battleship Potemkin
5	Greed*
6	Senso/Wanton Contessa*
7	M
8	Viridiana*
9	La Règle du Jeu/ The Rules of the Game*
10	O Thiassos/ The Travelling Players

GUILLERMO CABRERA INFANTE

BORN: 1929

Guillermo Cabrera Infante, the Cuban novelist, describes himself as 'movie critic once; screenwriter twice; a fan forever'. His choice is in no particular order.

Citizen Kane*
In a Lonely Place
Kiss Me Deadly
The Band Wagon*
The Searchers*
To Be or Not to Be*
The Woman in the Window
Vertigo*
Sunset Boulevard
Bladerunner

FIRST MOVIE: My mother turned me on to movies: she took me to see my first feature film when I was 29 days old. *Scarface* did the rest.
FIRST FILM WALKED OUT OF/
LEAST FAVOURITE MOVIE: *Chapayev*.
COMMENT: Why just 10 movies? Why not 20, 100, 100,000? Now in the winter of our content we all are, as Langlois loved to say, a cinematheque of the mind.

JAMES CARD
BORN: 1915

James Card is Director of the International Film League (East Rochester, New York). A distinguished writer and film historian, he has been important in the rediscovery of silent films. His list is in no particular order.

8½/Otto e Mezzo*
Bicycle Thieves/The Bicycle Thief/ Ladri di Biciclette
Fröken Julie/Miss Julie
Das Kabinett Des Dr Caligari/ The Cabinet of Dr Caligari*
La Passion de Jeanne d'Arc/ The Passion of Joan of Arc*
The Gold Rush*
Last Command
Kurutta Ippeni/Page Out of Order
City Girl
Olympische Spiele/Olympia

PETER CARGIN
BORN: 1943

Peter Cargin is Information Officer at the British Film Institute and Editor of *Film*; he is also Treasurer and Awards Organizer of the Critics' Circle Film Awards and Vice-President of the International Critics Association. His list is presented in alphabetical order.

The Band Wagon*
The Big Sleep
Charulata/The Lonely Wife
Claire's Knee/Le Genou de Claire*
The Cameraman
La Nuit Américaine/Day for Night
Le Charme Discret de la Bourgeoisie/ The Discreet Charm of the Bourgeoisie*
Midnight
Rio Bravo
Trouble in Paradise

FIRST MOVIE: *Count Three and Pray* (Sherman)
FIRST MOVIE WALKED OUT OF/
LEAST FAVOURITE MOVIE: *The Tea House of the August Moon* (Mann).

LILIANA CAVANI
BORN: 1938

Liliana Cavani is an Italian director whose films include *Night Encounter* (1961), *Francis of Asisi* (1966), *Il Portiere di Notte/The Night Porter* (1974) and *Beyond Evil* (1977).

1	City Lights*
2	Bicycle Thieves/ The Bicycle Thief/ Ladri di Biciclette*
3	Umberto D
4	Bellissima
5	Accattone
6	The Birds
7	Dr Strangelove
8	2001: A Space Odyssey*
9	Andrei Rublev*
10	The Servant

FIRST MOVIE: *Ordet/The Word* (Dreyer)
FIRST FILM WALKED OUT OF/
LEAST FAVOURITE MOVIE: *La Corona di Ferro* (Blasetti).
COMMENT: De Sica is one of the biggest movie directors. He is ignored by American critics and audiences. It is like ignoring Chekhov.

The story of the cinema in the form it has been written is incorrect. Cinema is like literature – it is the literature of the present and of the future. My opinion is that a lot of European directors are [the equivalents of] Proust, Mann and Balzac.

IAN CHRISTIE
BORN: 1927

Ian Christie is film critic for the *Daily Express* (London).

1	Citizen Kane*
2	Some Like It Hot*
3	Kind Hearts and Coronets*
4	The Wild Bunch
5	The Hustler
6	Ace in the Hole
7	Sunset Boulevard
8	The Maltese Falcon*
9	Charley Varrick
10	Casablanca*

FIRST MOVIE: A Tom Mix Western at a Saturday matinee
FIRST FILM WALKED OUT OF/
LEAST FAVOURITE MOVIE: The horror film I saw last week.

MICHEL CIMENT
BORN: 1938

Michel Ciment is a member of the editorial board of *Positif* and Associate Professor at the University of Paris where he teaches courses on American cinema. He has produced various books and films on cinema people and genres. His list combines admiration and pleasure and is in chronological order.

The Navigator*
Sunrise*
L'Atalante*
La Règle du Jeu/The Rules of the Game*
Wagonmaster
Singin' in the Rain*
Sansho the Bailiff/Sansho Dayu*
Madame De . . ./ The Earrings of Madame De . . ./ Diamond Earrings*
Persona
Roma

FIRST MOVIE: I don't remember but (I hope) it may very well have been a Michael Curtiz/Errol Flynn swashbuckler; *A Man Escaped* and *Lola Montez*, which I saw before the age of 20, made me conscious of film language.
FIRST FILM WALKED OUT OF/
LEAST FAVOURITE MOVIE: I don't remember but it could very well be Jean-Marie Straub's *Othon*.

LORENZO CODELLI
BORN: 1946

Lorenzo Codelli is the editor of various books and catalogues; an organizer of the Pordenone Silent Film Festival (Italy); a contributor to *Positif, Ekran, Filméchange* and other magazines; and a correspondent of *The International Film Guide*. His list is in alphabetical order.

The Conversation
La Famiglia Passaguai
The Far Country*
Heaven Can Wait
The Honey Pot
Lolita
Manhattan*
Some Like It Hot*
Unfaithfully Yours
The Wedding March

FIRST MOVIE: Disney cartoons, Laurel and Hardy comedies and MGM musicals.
FIRST FILM WALKED OUT OF/
LEAST FAVOURITE MOVIE: A scary Totò farce probably.
COMMENT: *The Conversation*, or the Spirit of the Seventies, fears and desires, dreams and deceptions; Aldo Fabrizi's *La Familia Passaguai* and its sequel, Fabrizi's *La Famiglia Passaguai Fa Fortuna* – roots of Italian popular cinema; Anthony Mann's *The Far Country* – the space-opera; Lubitsch's *Heaven Can Wait* – waltz as life, or vice versa; von Stronheim's *The Wedding March* – Genius and Folly, a whole Empire rebuilt.

RICHARD COMBS
BORN: 1947

Richard Combs lives in London and is editor of *Monthly Film Bulletin*, staff contributor to *Sight and Sound*, weekly columnist in *The Listener*, contributor to various newspapers, periodicals and partworks on the cinema, and co-author of *Robert Aldrich*. He has taught and lectured at the Royal College of Art and National Film Theatre. His list is in alphabetical order.

Altman's Desert Cycle (Three Women; Come Back to the Five and Dime, Jimmy Dean, Jimmy Dean)
Barry Lyndon
Dream Street
Le Feu Follet/Will of the Wisp
The Immortal Story
The Lightship
Seven Women
Signs of Life/Lebenszeichen*
La Décade Prodigieuse/ Ten Days' Wonder
Ulzana's Raid

FIRST MOVIE: *Torn Curtain* (Hitchcock), *Seven Women* (Ford), *Il Bidone* (Fellini), all seen in the late 1960s and which proved, in various ways, and regardless of ten-best ratings, eye-opening experiences.
LEAST FAVOURITE MOVIE: Harder to sort out the legion of candidates than with ten-best films; recently *The Killing Fields*, or generally something starring David Niven or Anthony Quinn.

CALLISTO COSULICH
BORN: 1922

Callisto Cosulich is an Italian film critic. His list is in alphabetical order.

Ai-No Corrida/Empire of the Senses*
Heimat*
Ivan the Terrible Parts I and II/ Ivan Groznyi*
Land des Schweigens und der Dunkelheit/ Land of Silence and Darkness
The Long Voyage Home
Monsieur Verdoux*
Paisà/Paisan*
The Scarlet Empress*
Tokyo Story/Tokyo Monogatari*
Ugetsu Monogatari*

FIRST MOVIE: *Manon Lescaut* (Robinson).
FIRST FILM WALKED OUT OF/
LEAST FAVOURITE MOVIE: None.

VIRGINIA DIGNAM

BORN: at 5am on the 25th day of the 5th month of a year when there was still £ s d Virginia Dignam is a British actress, critic, writer about films, interviewer, enthusiastic filmgoer and mother of four children, three of whom have appeared in films.

1	Les Enfants du Paradis/ Children of Paradise*
2	Battleship Potemkin/ Bronenosets Potyomkin*
3	Viridiana*
4	The Third Man*
5	Kind Hearts and Coronets*
6	A King in New York
7	Bicycle Thieves/ The Bicycle Thief/ Ladri di Biciclette*
8	Raba Lubvi/Slave of Love
9	The African Queen*
10	Mean Streets

FIRST MOVIE: Chaplin films at which I laughed and cried as a small child, always feeling protective towards Charlie.
FIRST FILM WALKED OUT OF/
LEAST FAVOURITE MOVIE: All horror films.

CZESLAW DONDZILLO

BORN: 1942

Czeslaw Dondzillo, a Polish film critic, is Editor-in-chief of *Film* illustrated magazine.

1	Citizen Kane*
2	Battleship Potemkin/ Bronenosets Potyomkin*
3	Some Like It Hot*
4	High Noon
5	One Flew Over The Cuckoo's Nest*
6	Sud 'ba Tcheloveka/Destiny of a Man
7	Rashomon*
8	La Grande Illusion/ Grand Illusion*
9	The Birds
10	Wild Strawberries/ Smultronstället*

FIRST MOVIE: A few of Bergman's first films. I was also interested in Polish films of the late 1950s.
FIRST FILM WALKED OUT OF/
LEAST FAVOURITE MOVIE: French comedies, especially those made in the 1970s.

WOLF DONNER

BORN: 1939

Wolf Donner is Editor of the West German ARD-TV arts programme *Titel, Thesen Temperamente*, Film and TV Editor of the weekly *Die Zeit*, Director of the Berlin International Film Festival, Co-director of the cultural department of *Der Spiegel* and is a film critic for various magazines and TV programmes.

1	Citizen Kane*
2	La Règle du Jeu/ The Rules of the Game*
3	Modern Times*
4	2001: A Space Odyssey*
5	La Dolce Vita*
6	Wild Strawberries/ Smultronstället*
7	Stalker
8	Casablanca*
9	Rebel without a Cause
10	Lawrence of Arabia*

FIRST MOVIE: *Sunrise* (Murnau).
FIRST FILM WALKED OUT OF/
LEAST FAVOURITE MOVIE: Any Jerry Lewis film.

RAYMOND DURGNAT

BORN: 1932

Raymond Durgnat, the distinguished British film writer, is Visiting Professor in Film Studies at UCLA, UC Berkeley, UC San Diego, Columbia NYC, Dartmouth College NH, University of Oklahoma, San Francisco State and other American universities. His list is in no particular order.

Yellow Submarine
Ruby Gentry
Look Back in Anger
Tirez sur le Pianiste/ Shoot the Pianist
Miraculo a Milano/Miracle in Milan
Leo the Last
Saps at Sea
L'Atalante*
French Can-Can
Hellzapoppin

FIRST MOVIE: *The Thief of Bagdad* (Powell/Whelan/Berger).
LEAST FAVOURITE MOVIE: Any Ratycal-dogmatic-Marxist-Formalist British movie!
COMMENT: As I've been teaching film largely through close analysis for nearly thirty years, I really have seen some of these films thirty or forty times, image by image, while discussing every move in them with classroomfuls (from 5 to 300) of students – some touchingly keen, some highly rude – and these films, however many times you analyse them to death, miraculously spring alive again . . .

CARL HUBERT FELIX
BORN: 1961

Carl Hubert Felix is a Belgian film critic.

1	Eraserhead
2	Freaks*
3	ZOO
4	The Seventh Seal/ Det Sjunde Inseglet*
5	The Maltese Falcon*
6	Brazil
7	Tagebuch einer Verlorenen/ Diary of a Lost Girl
8	Touch of Evil*
9	M
10	The Incredible Shrinking Man

FIRST MOVIE: I remember the magic of Walt Disney's movies when I was a kid, and the charm of Sci-fi movies of the 1950s which I saw on TV.

FIRST FILM WALKED OUT OF/
LEAST FAVOURITE MOVIE: Impossible to say. Even in the worst film, there is always a tiny little something. Sometimes you have to search for it a little deeper, that's all!

ANGEL FERNÁNDEZ-SANTOS
BORN: 1934

Angel Fernández-Santos is a Spanish screenwriter (*El Espíritu de la Colmena, Padre Nuestro, Diario de Invierno*), writer (*Mas Allá del Oeste, Maiakovski y el cine*) and film critic for *El Pais*.

1	Sunrise*
2	Ordet/The Word*
3	The Searchers*
4	Rear Window
5	La Règle du Jeu/ The Rules of the Game*
6	Sansho the Bailiff/ Sansho Dayu*
7	Touch of Evil*
8	Octjabr/October
9	Germania, Anno Zero/ Germany, Year Zero
10	Limelight

FIRST MOVIE: *How Green Was My Valley* (Ford).

PHILIP FRENCH
BORN: 1933

Philip French has been film critic for the *Observer* (London) since 1978 and contributes on the cinema for numerous papers and magazines. He is the author of *The Movie Moguls* and *Westerns* and in 1986 was a member of the Cannes Film Festival Jury. His list is in chronological order.

Battleship Potemkin/ Bronenosets Potyomkin*
The General*
The Lady Vanishes*
Stagecoach*
La Règle du Jeu/ The Rules of the Game*
Citizen Kane*
Singin' in the Rain*
The Seven Samurai/ Shichinin No Samurai*
Wild Strawberries/Smultronstället*
Salvatore Giuliano

FIRST MOVIE: Possibly *Snow White* in 1938 or *The Four Feathers* in the following year, though these were preceded by unidentifiable B-feature Westerns and adventure flicks.

FIRST FILM WALKED OUT OF/
LEAST FAVOURITE MOVIE: Impossible to answer; besides, I do not bear grudges.

JUAN CARLOS FRUGONE
BORN: 1938

Juan Carlos Frugone is film correspondent for the Buenos Aires *Clarin*; Deputy Director (since 1984) of the Valladolid Film Festival; author of *Mario Camus* (Spanish director) and *Rafel Azcona* (Spanish screenwriter); film critic for many Spanish papers and magazines; Secretary-General of the Latin American Film Festival in Huelva (1979-81) and a member of several other international film festival juries.

1	Casablanca*
2	Manhattan*
3	That's Entertainment Part I
4	A Star Is Born (1954)
5	Viskningar och Rop/ Cries and Whispers
6	Jules et Jim*
7	The Beguiled
8	Funny Face
9	The Magnificent Ambersons
10	Freaks*

COMMENT: I want to remark that my list doesn't include what I think are perhaps 'The Best' or 'The Most Important' films in the history of cinema. I have only chosen those I've seen many times and which I would be able to see many times again.

PENELOPE GILLIATT
BORN: 1933

Penelope Gilliatt, the British novelist, has been film critic for the *New Yorker* and *Observer*. As a screenwriter she won several awards, including an Oscar nomination, for *Sunday Bloody Sunday*.

1	The Navigator*
2	La Règle du Jeu/ The Rules of the Game*
3	Zéro de Conduite/ Zero for Conduct*
4	8½/Otto e Mezzo*
5	Apu Trilogy*
6	Ikiru/Living*
7	Some Like It Hot*
8	Jules et Jim*
9	She Wore a Yellow Ribbon
10	Dr Strangelove

FIRST MOVIE: *Birth of a Nation* (Griffith) in full length with my nursemaid when I was 7. She thought it was about the babyhood of great English prime ministers.
FIRST FILM WALKED OUT OF/
LEAST FAVOURITE MOVIE: *Bambi* (Disney).

GIOVANNI GRAZZINI
BORN: 1925

Giovanni Grazzini is film critic for *Corriere della Sera* (Milan) and President of the Centro Sperimentale di Cinematografia in Rome.

1	Modern Times*
2	Intolerance
3	Battleship Potemkin/ Bronenosets Potyomkin*
4	Metropolis
5	La Grande Illusion/ Grand Illusion*
6	Stagecoach*
7	Citizen Kane*
8	Paisà/Paisan*
9	8½/Otto e Mezzo*
10	Andrei Rublev*

FIRST MOVIE: *Leise Flehen Meine Lieder* (Forst).
FIRST FILM WALKED OUT OF/
LEAST FAVOURITE MOVIE: *Othos* (Straub).

ULRICH GREGOR
BORN: 1932

Ulrich Gregor is co-author with Enno Patalas of *History of Cinema* and author of *History of Cinema since 1960*, Co-founder of Friends of the German Film Archive and, since 1971, Director of the International Forum of Young Cinema. His list is in no particular order.

La Terra Trema*
Paisà/Paisan*
Battleship Potemkin/ Bronenosets Potyomkin*
Wavelength
Nosferatu (Murnau)
Andrei Rublev*
La Maman et la Putain/ The Mother and the Whore
Im Lauf der Zeit/Kings of the Road
Apa/Father
Citizen Kane*

FIRST MOVIE: *Ladri di Biciclette/Bicycle Thieves* (De Sica).

JOSE LUIS GUARNER
BORN: 1937

Jose Luis Guarner is a film critic for *Fotogramas* and *La Vanguardia*, author of monographs on Rossellini, Visconti and Pasolini, and President of the Barcelona Film Festival. His list is in alphabetical order.

Bringing Up Baby*
The General*
Johnny Guitar
Modern Times*
The Searchers*
Singin' in the Rain*
The Thief of Bagdad*
The Third Man*
Touch of Evil*
Vertigo*

FIRST MOVIE: *High Noon* (Zinnemann).
FIRST FILM WALKED OUT OF/
LEAST FAVOURITE MOVIE: I have almost never walked out of a movie.

MANUEL HIDALGO
BORN: 1953

Manuel Hidalgo has been film critic for the Madrid daily paper *Diano 16* since 1982 and contributor to *Cambio 16* and *Fotogramas*. He is the author of six books on Spanish actors and directors. His first novel *El pecador impecable* was adapted for the screen in 1987, the same year in which he was a member of the Cannes Film Festival jury.

1 The Man Who Shot Liberty Valance
2 La Passion de Jeanne d'Arc/ The Passion of Joan of Arc*
3 Bicycle Thieves/ The Bicycle Thief/ Ladri di Biciclette*
4 Citizen Kane*
5 Bringing Up Baby*
6 Touch of Evil*
7 Viaggio in Italia/ Voyage to Italy/ The Divorce of Naples/ The Greatest Love/ Love is the Strongest/ The Lonely Wife*
8 The Night of the Hunter
9 Johnny Guitar
10 A Place in the Sun

FIRST MOVIE: *L'Avventura* (Antonioni).
FIRST FILM WALKED OUT OF/
LEAST FAVOURITE MOVIE: *A Night at the Opera* (Wood).

GILLES JACOB
BORN: 1930

Gilles Jacob was a film critic for 13 years. He is currently Director of Cannes Film Festival.

1 Citizen Kane*
2 La Règle du Jeu/ The Rules of the Game*
3 The Gold Rush*
4 Sunrise*
5 Foolish Wives
6 8½/Otto e Mezzo*
7 Wild Strawberries/ Smultronstället*
8 Louisiana Story
9 The General*
10 Battleship Potemkin/ Bronenosets Potyomkin*

FIRST MOVIE: *L'Homme du Niger*.
FIRST FILM WALKED OUT OF/
LEAST FAVOURITE MOVIE: *Vautrin*.

ALBERT JOHNSON
BORN: 1900

Albert Johnson is the former director of the San Francisco Film Festival. His list is in no particular order.

The Best Years of Our Lives*
Citizen Kane*
City Lights*
Mirror/Zemlya*
Farrébique
Henry V
Der Letzte Mann/The Last Laugh
Notti di Cabiria/Cabiria/ Nights of Cabiria*
Voina i Mir/War and Peace
Apu Trilogy*

IAIN JOHNSTONE
BORN: 1953

Iain Johnstone is film critic for the *Sunday Times* (London).

1 A Fish Called Wanda
2 Claire's Knee/ Le Genou de Claire*
3 Ma Nuit Chez Maud/ My Night with Maud
4 The Bridge on the River Kwai
5 Chushingura/The 47 Ronin
6 Maz Swojej Zony/ His Wife's Husband
7 L'Avventura*
8 Play Misty for Me
9 The Godfather
10 The Graduate

FIRST FILM WALKED OUT OF/
LEAST FAVOURITE MOVIE: *King Lear* (Brook).

RENE JORDAN
BORN: 1928

Rene Jordan reviewed films for *Excelsior* and *Bohemia* magazine in Cuba until 1960. He now writes for *El Miami Herald*, Spanish section and *Cosmopolitan in Spanish*. He is the author of biographies of Gable, Brando, Cooper and Streisand.

1	Citizen Kane*
2	La Règle du Jeu/ The Rules of the Game*
3	Madame De . . ./ The Earrings of Madame De .../ Diamond Earrings*
4	Vertigo*
5	8½/Otto e Mezzo*
6	L'Avventura*
7	Jules et Jim*
8	Brief Encounter*
9	Tokyo Story/ Tokyo Monogatari*
10	Close Encounters of the Third Kind

FIRST MOVIE: Norma Shearer in *Smilin' Through* (Franklin) at age three or four. After that – as an addict – they all impressed me.
FIRST FILM WALKED OUT OF/
LEAST FAVOURITE MOVIE: The one I saw three hours ago: Oliver Stone's *Wall Street*.

TULLIO KEZICH
BORN: 1928

Tullio Zezich is film critic for the Rome daily *La Repubblica* and for *Panorama*. In the 1960s he produced films in association with Ermanno Olmi. He has written various books on the movies and a recent biography, *Fellini*.

1	Stagecoach*
2	Bicycle Thieves/ The Bicycle Thief/ Ladri di Biciclette*
3	Grand Illusion/ La Grande Illusion*
4	8½/Otto e Mezzo*
5	2001: A Space Odyssey*
6	Sacrificatio/Offret/ The Sacrifice*
7	Wild Strawberries/ Smultronstället*
8	Modern Times*
9	The Band Wagon*
10	M

FIRST MOVIE: *The Singing Fool* (Bacon) with Al Jolson.
FIRST FILM WALKED OUT OF/
LEASE FAVOURITE MOVIE: *Portrait of Jennie* (Dieterle).

ALEKSANDER KUKARKIN
BORN: 1916

Aleksander Kukarkin is a Moscow film critic.

1	City Lights*
2	Chapayev
3	Gone with the Wind*
4	Wild Strawberries/ Smultronstället*
5	Cabaret
6	Andrei Rublev*
7	The Best Years of Our Lives*
8	Citizen Kane*
9	Sous les Toits de Paris/ Under the Roofs of Paris
10	Roma, Città Aperta/ Rome, Open City*

FIRST MOVIE: *The Gold Rush* (Chaplin).
FIRST FILM WALKED OUT OF/
LEAST FAVOURITE MOVIE: There are too many of them.

KYUSHIRO KUSAKABE
BORN: 1920

Kyushiro Kusakabe was a film critic for Mainichi Newspapers from 1948 to 1978. In 1980 he founded the Japan Image Arts Co. and in 1984 was Director of the Tokyo International Film Festival. He has also been a member of the Berlin (1967), Kracow (1981) and Red Cross (1987) Film Festival juries.

1	La Grande Illusion/ Grand Illusion*
2	Les Enfants du Paradis/ Children of Paradise*
3	Roma, Città Aperta/ Rome, Open City*
4	L'Année Dernière à Marienbad/ Last Year at Marienbad*
5	8½/Otto e Mezzo*
6	Limelight
7	Lawrence of Arabia*
8	2001: A Space Odyssey*
9	Pierrot Le Fou*
10	Rashomon*

FIRST MOVIE: *Morroco* (von Sternberg).
FIRST FILM WALKED OUT OF/
LEAST FAVOURITE MOVIE: *Le Quatorze Juillet* (Clair).

MICHAEL J. KUTZA
BORN: 1939

Michael J. Kutza is the founder and artistic director of the Chicago International Film Festival (now in its 24th year). He is also the film critic for *Il Tempo (Rom)*.

1	Citizen Kane*
2	2001: A Space Odyssey*
3	Singin' in the Rain*
4	City Lights*
5	Fantasia
6	Fanny and Alexander/ Fanny och Alexander*
7	Veronika Voss
8	Cabaret
9	The Wizard of Oz*
10	A Star Is Born (1954)

FIRST MOVIE: (A double bill) *Bambi* and *Abbott and Costello Meet Frankenstein.*
FIRST FILM WALKED OUT OF/
LEAST FAVOURITE MOVIE: *The Legend of Lila Claire, The Mission, 1941, Perfect, Star!*

JOHN FRANCIS LANE
BORN: 1928

John Francis Lane, who has lived in Rome since the early 1950s, was Italian correspondent for *Films and Filming* until the 1970s, contributed to *Sight and Sound*, *The Times* and the *Guardian* among others and has been Rome correspondent of *Screen International* since 1984.

1	Senso/Wanton Contessa*
2	La Terra Trema*
3	La Dolce Vita/The Sweet Life*
4	Citizen Kane*
5	Wild Strawberries/ Smultronstället*
6	L'Avventura*
7	Le Règle du Jeu/ The Rules of the Game*
8	Rashomon*
9	2001: A Space Odyssey*
10	Le Charme Discret de la Bourgeoisie/The Discreet Charm of the Bourgeoisie*

FIRST MOVIE: *The Great Ziegfeld* (Leonard).
FIRST FILM WALKED OUT OF/
LEAST FAVOURITE MOVIE: *Helzapoppin* (Potter).
COMMENT: These are all films I've watched on TV and no film made since 1970 seems to me to be better. I'm sorry not to have included *Casablanca* which was a cult movie for my generation before cult movies were invented.

ANN LLOYD
BORN: 1945

Ann Lloyd lives in London. She has edited many film books and was Editor of the weekly partwork magazine *The Movie*. She is also a freelance writer and film reviewer. Her list is in chronological order.

The Gold Rush*
Marius Trilogy
To Be or Not to Be*
Apu Trilogy*
Les Amants/The Lovers
The Innocents
Kwaidan
The Harder They Come
Xala
The Warriors

FIRST MOVIE: *Dumbo* (Disney).
FIRST FILM WALKED OUT OF/
LEAST FAVOURITE MOVIE: *The Belly of an Architect* (Greenaway) was the last film I walked out of.
COMMENT: I thought long and hard about why so few American or English films featured in this list. I think they too often lack a sensuousness that I would especially need on a desert island. And nothing since 1979!

JACQUES LOURCELLES
BORN: 1940

Jacques Lourcelles lives in Paris where he edits a cinema magazine. He is the author of books and articles on films and is a screenwriter.

1	While the City Sleeps
2	Forever Amber
3	The Life of O-Haru/ Saikaku Ichidai Onna*
4	Objective Burma
5	Cat People
6	Psycho*
7	Silver Lode
8	Faisons un Rêve
9	The Far Country*
10	The Bells of St Mary's

FIRST MOVIE: *The Cure* (Chaplin).
FIRST FILM WALKED OUT OF/
LEAST FAVOURITE MOVIE: *Hiroshima Mon Amour* (Resnais).

AZZEDINE MABROUKI
BORN: 1946

Azzedine Mabrouke is a journalist and film critic for *El Moudjahid* (daily), *Algérie Actualité* (weekly) and *Parcours Maghrébim* (monthly) in Algeria and for *7ième Art* in Tunisia. He is a member of FIPRECI (Fédération Internationale de la Presse Cinématographique).

1	Sayat Nova/ The Colour of Pomegranates
2	Apu Trilogy*
3	Citizen Kane*
4	Bezhin Lug/Bezhin Meadow
5	The Barefoot Contessa
6	Antonia das Mortes
7	Gare Centrale/Central Station
8	Passion
9	O Thiassos/ The Travelling Players
10	The Shanghai Gesture

FIRST MOVIE: *La Mère* (Poudovkine).
FIRST FILM WALKED OUT OF/
LEAST FAVOURITE MOVIE: *Rambo*!
COMMENT: I honestly believe that *Sayat Nova* (Parazdanov) is the best film I have seen in my life. Second: the work of Satyajit Ray (*Apu's World*).◄

FRANCES LYNN

Frances Lynn lives in London. She has contributed film criticism to several magazines including *Showbiz*, *Film Review* and *Screen International*. She was also film critic for *Movie Star* (under a pseudonym) and wrote the original film treatment for Don Boyd's *Gossip*. From 1976 to 1986 she was Film Editor on *Ritz* newspaper and she is currently writing a screenplay.

1	The Night of the Living Dead/ The Night of the Flesh Eaters*
2	Beyond the Valley of the Dolls
3	Phantom of the Paradise
4	Suspiria
5	Giuletta degli Spiriti/ Juliet of the Spirits
6	The Women
7	Das Kabinett Des Dr Caligari/ The Cabinet of Dr Caligari*
8	Orphée
9	Videodrome
10	Rosemary's Baby

FIRST MOVIE: *The Lady and the Tramp* (Disney) when I was five years old.
FIRST FILM WALKED OUT OF/
LEAST FAVOURITE MOVIE: *Ishtar*.
COMMENT: Out of my ten favourite movies, *The Night of the Living Dead* tops the list because it is the only horror film I have passed out in – screaming and coming to in the aisles of a San Francisco theatre at midnight on Halloween.

DEREK MALCOLM
BORN: 1932

Derek Malcolm has been film critic for the *Guardian* (London) since 1971 and *Cosmopolitan* UK since 1974. He was Director of the London Film Festival for the years 1984-6.

1	The Life of O'Haru/ Saikaku Ichidai Onna*
2	Samma no Aji/ An Autumn Afternoon
3	El
4	Madame De …/ The Earrings of Madame De …/ Diamond Earrings*
5	Touch of Evil*
6	Monsieur Verdoux*
7	Rio Bravo
8	Ikiru/Living*
9	Det Sjunde Inseglet/ The Seventh Seal*
10	Jalsaghar/The Music Room

FIRST MOVIE: Turned on by Korda's *The Private Life of Henry VIII*.
FIRST FILM WALKED OUT OF/
LEAST FAVOURITE MOVIE: Turned off by De Mille's *The Ten Commandments*.
COMMENT: There are great films I've seen so often that I'd rather not pursue them into boredom, like *Citizen Kane* and *Battleship Potemkin*.

LEONARD MALTIN
BORN: 1950

Since 1982 Leonard Maltin has been film correspondent for the American TV show *Entertainment Tonight*. His 11 books include *The Great Movie Comedians* and *The Art of the Cinematographer*. He is also Editor of the annual reference *Leonard Maltin's TV Movies and Video Guide*.

1	Casablanca*
2	The Maltese Falcon*
3	Citizen Kane*
4	Singin' in the Rain*
5	Modern Times*
6	A Night at the Opera
7	King Kong (1933)
8	It's a Wonderful Life
9	Dumbo
10	All the other great movies I forgot

FIRST MOVIE: A reissue of *Snow White and the Seven Dwarfs* – emphatically *not* the original release (I wasn't born yet!).
FIRST FILM WALKED OUT OF/
LEAST FAVOURITE MOVIE: Too many to name.
COMMENT: People ask me why I don't have more current movies on my list of favourites. It's not that I don't like contemporary films, but I find that I just can't muster the kind of *affection* for them that I feel towards the movies of the past. I also know that this may have something to do with not having the distance of time to cast a kind of glow on the newer films. Just the same, I can't picture ever changing this list very much in the future.

MARCEL MARTIN
BORN: 1926

Marcel Martin is a critic and film historian. He lives in Paris.

1 Les Enfants du Paradis/ Children of Paradise*
2 Hiroshima Mon Amour*
3 Ugetsu Monogatari*
4 Aleksandr Nevskii/ Alexander Nevsky*
5 Sunrise*
6 Viaggio in Italia/ Voyage to Italy/ The Divorcee of Naples/ The Greatest Love/ Love is the Strongest/ The Lonely Wife*
7 8½/Otto e Mezzo*
8 Jules et Jim*
9 Tokyo Story/Tokyo Monogatari*
10 Mirror/Zemlya*

FIRST MOVIE: *Test Pilot* (Fleming).

SIMON MIZRAHI
BORN 1940:

Simon Mizrahi was born in Egypt, went to film school in Paris and worked as actor and assistant director to Nicholas Ray and Anthony Mann in Spain. He has been a film editor in French TV and dubbing editor for the Cinematheque Française (1970-end 1971). He is now an independent press agent who has helped in the revival of interest in Italian films in France.

1 Moonfleet/Nature's Freaks/ Forbidden Love/ Nature's Mistress/ The Monster Show*
2 Saint Joan
3 Sea Devils
4 Night of the Demon
5 Sansho the Bailiff/ Sansho Dayu*
6 Lifeboat
7 Slightly Scarlet
8 Man of the West
9 An Affair to Remember
10 The Wings of Eagles

FIRST MOVIE: *Tarzan the Ape Man*, which I saw in Cairo at the age of 6.

LEAST FAVOURITE MOVIE: Antonioni's abominable *L'Avventura* and Resnais' unbearable *Hiroshima Mon Amour*.

COMMENT: To give one's list of 10 or 15 best films of all time makes no sense for a serious film buff. The best 100 would be more accurate . . .

HARUO MIZUNO
BORN: 1931

Haruo Mizuno appears on a Japanese TV movie programme three times a week. He also writes film reviews for various newspapers and magazines.

1 Gone with the Wind*
2 Casablanca*
3 The Third Man*
4 My Darling Clementine*
5 Citizen Kane*
6 The Best Years of Our Lives*
7 All about Eve
8 North by Northwest
9 La Grande Illusion/ Grand Illusion*
10 Les Jeux Interdits/ Forbidden Games

FIRST MOVIE: *Gone with the Wind.*

KAZIMIERZ MLYNARZ
BORN: 1933

Kazimierz Mlynarz is Editor-in-chief and film critic of the Polish monthly *Nurt*. Since 1955 he has been an active member of the Polish ciné-clubs movement and since 1965 a member of the Polish Council of Art Movies. He was a lecturer in film studies at the University of Poznań, 1977-81. He is also the translator and editor of three editions of a Polish selection of Bergman's screenplays.

1 Wild Strawberries/ Smultronstället*
2 The Seven Samurai/ Shichinin No Samurai*
3 8½/Otto e Mezzo*
4 The Gold Rush*
5 Ivan the Terrible Parts I and II/ Ivan Groznyi*
6 Andrei Rublev*
7 Ashes and Diamonds/ Popiół i Diament*
8 2001: A Space Odyssey*
9 Viridiana*
10 Il Gattopardo/The Leopard

FIRST MOVIE: *White Fang* (Zguridi).
FIRST FILM WALKED OUT OF/
LEAST FAVOURITE MOVIE: *Jud Süss* (Harlan).
COMMENT: Thank American cinematography for the Western, which is not only the most popular film genre: it is our dreamland.

KHALID MOHAMED
BORN: 1953

Khalid Mohamed is a film critic and feature writer for *The Times of India*. he also writes on film for various Indian publications and interviews film personalities for television. His list is in no particular order.

Pierrot le Fou

Une Femme Douce/
A Gentle Creature

Dodeska Den

Die Bitteren Tränen der Petra von Kant/The Bitter Tears of Petra von Kant

Deep End

Aranyer din Pratidwandi/
Siddhartha and the City

Mughal-e-Azam/The Great Mogul

110.5Taxi Driver

Some Like It Hot*

Signs of Life/Lebenszeichen*

FIRST MOVIE: A fairy-tale, *Hatim Tai*, made for the Indian cinema; and Jerry Lewis' *Rock-a-Bye-Baby* for the rest.
FIRST FILM WALKED OUT OF/
LEAST FAVOURITE MOVIE: *Sammy and Rosie Get Laid*.
COMMENT: After months of mulling, fretting, going bananas, I decided to opt for spontaneity rather than sense. So the list is made on a Monday morning in a rush . . . The films selected have been based on sentimental moments spent in the dark, for the small tear shed and for the loud cackle of laughter that made the person in the next seat see red. They are films without which living wouldn't have been the same.

SHERIDAN MORLEY
BORN: 1941

Sheridan Morley has been Arts Editor and drama critic of *Punch* (London) since 1975; he wrote and presented the television series *Film Night* in 1971/72; wrote the TV movies column of *Radio Times* in the 1970s and of the *Mail on Sunday* in the 1980s. He is the son and grandson and godson of actors who worked in movies.

1	Jules et Jim*
2	Casablanca*
3	Napoléon*
4	Beat the Devil
5	The Band Wagon*
6	Brief Encounter*
7	Henry V
8	The Front
9	Rebecca*
10	42nd Street

FIRST MOVIE: *The Wizard of Oz*, largely for Garland and the moment when black and white became colour.
FIRST FILM WALKED OUT OF/
LEAST FAVOURITE MOVIE: *Rocky* (I through IV), anything featuring dancing female welders (cf. *Breakdance*).

SWAPAN MULLICK
BORN: 1947

Swapan Mullick is film critic for the Calcutta *New Statesman*. He won the National Award for Best Film Journalist of India in 1985 and has attended major international film festivals.

1	Citizen Kane*
2	Akahige/Red Beard
3	Battleship Potemkin/ Bronenosets Potyomkin*
4	Modern Times*
5	Stagecoach*
6	Strangers on a Train
7	Rashomon*
8	Wild Strawberries/ Smultronstället*
9	Apur Sansar/The World of Apu*
10	Gone with the Wind*

FIRST MOVIE: *Citizen Kane*.
FIRST FILM WALKED OUT OF/
LEAST FAVOURITE MOVIE: *The Godfather* (Coppola).
COMMENT: A difficult choice. So I seized on the simplest method: I asked myself which were the films I'd seen four times each already, and which were the films I'd like to keep while serving a sentence of house confinement for bad writing! The list emerged gradually but left me gasping for more.

HEINZ NIEMANN
BORN: 1930

Heinz Niemann, who is based in Berlin, has been a film critic since 1953 and correspondent for the Tokyo monthly *Movie/TV Marketing* since 1969. He was Head of the Feature Film Department, TV GDR from 1973 to 1979. He has recently contributed a chapter on the Hungarian film theoretician and writer Béla Balázs in *Berliner Begegnungen* (1987). His list is in chronological order.

The Gold Rush*

Potomok Tshingis-khana/
The Heir to Ghengis Khan

Twelve Angry Men

Andrei Rublev*

Blow-up

Abschied/Farewell

La Nuit Américaine/Day for Night

Ana y los Lobos/
Anna and the Wolves

Lancelot du Lac

1900

FIRST MOVIE: Laurel and Hardy; definitely the first I'd seen.
FIRST FILM WALKED OUT OF/
LEAST FAVOURITE MOVIE: There are too many.

MICHAEL PARKINSON

BORN: 1935

Michael Parkinson lives in England. He wrote and presented the television series *Cinema*, was guest presenter of *Film 87* (BBC TV), chairman of *The Movie Quiz* (BBC TV) and co-author with Clyde Jeavons of *Pictorial History of the Western*. His list is in no particular order.

1. The Gold Rush*
2. Singin' in the Rain*
3. Butch Cassidy and the Sundance Kid
4. The Seven Samurai/ Shichinin No Samurai*
5. Casablanca*
6. Broadway Danny Rose
7. Raiders of the Lost Ark
8. Destry Rides Again
9. On the Waterfront
10. Monsieur Hulot's Holiday

FIRST MOVIE: Chaplin shorts; Laurel and Hardy; The Three Stooges.
FIRST FILM WALKED OUT OF/
LEAST FAVOURITE MOVIE: Any film by Derek Jarman.

GEORGE PERRY

BORN: 1935

George Perry is the author of a number of books on the cinema, including *The Great British Picture Show*, *Forever Ealing* and *Hitchcock*. In 1970 he was Director of Cinema City. Currently he is Films Editor of the *Sunday Times*, film critic for *Illustrated London News* and Vice-Chairman of the Critics' Circle Film Section.

1. Singin' in the Rain*
2. Citizen Kane*
3. La Grande Illusion/ Grand Illusion*
4. The Third Man*
5. Lawrence of Arabia*
6. Kind Hearts and Coronets*
7. Top Hat
8. Strangers on a Train
9. 2001: A Space Odyssey*
10. The Life and Death of Colonel Blimp

FIRST MOVIE: *The Prisoner of Zenda* (Cromwell).
FIRST FILM WALKED OUT OF/
LEAST FAVOURITE MOVIE: *Myra Breckinridge* (Sarne).

AUDREY PLAKHOV

BORN: 1950

Audrey Plakhov is a Moscow film critic and Secretary of the Board USSR Filmmakers Union.

1. La Caduta degli Dei/ The Damned
2. La Règle du Jeu/ The Rules of the Game*
3. La Passion de Jeanne d'Arc/ The Passion of Joan of Arc*
4. Rashomon*
5. Wild Strawberries/ Smultronstället*
6. Mirror/Zemlya*
7. Belle de Jour
8. Ashes and Diamond/ Popiól i Diament*
9. Jules et Jim*
10. La Strada*

FIRST MOVIE: *L'Eclisse* (Antonioni)
FIRST FILM WALKED OUT OF/
LEAST FAVOURITE MOVIE: There are a lot of worthless films. I love cinema too much to concentrate my attention on antipathies.
COMMENT: My choice is more than subjective, as I cannot rank myself among connoisseurs of old and 'exotic' cinema. But not including many traditionally famous pictures of 1910–30 is deliberate. If one approaches cinema not as a subject of historical-structural research, but as a sphere of aesthetic experience, I prefer not early but mature cinema, in spite of its current crisis situation.

JERZY PLAZEWSKI

BORN: 1924

Dr Jerzy Plazewski is a Polish film historian and critic; Foreign Editor of the monthly *Kino*; Artistic Director of 'Cinema of Good Films Wiedza' in Warsaw; author of 14 books about films including *History of World Cinema for Everyone* and *Language of Film*. He is Vice-Chairman of the Polish Section of FIPRESCI; an officer on the Committee for the Purchasing of Foreign Films; a member of the Cannes, Berlin, Istanbul and Acapulco film festival juries.

1. Citizen Kane*
2. Battleship Potemkin/ Bronenosets Potemkin*
3. 8½/Otto e Mezzo*
4. The Sacrifice/Sacrificatio*
5. Rashomon*
6. Roma, Città Aperta/ Rome, Open City*
7. The Gold Rush*
8. Ashes and Diamonds/ Popiól i Diament*
9. Providence
10. Les Enfants du Paradis/ Children of Paradise*

FIRST MOVIE: *La Grande Illusion/Grand Illusion* (Renoir) in 1938.
LEAST FAVOURITE MOVIE: If I understand this correctly and you mean 'an important but overrated movie', then *Le Million* (Clair).

T. M. RAMACHANDRAN
BORN: 1920

T. M. Ramachandran, who lives in Bombay, has been a film critic since 1937; Cinema Editor for *The Hindu* and *Sport and Pastime* (1937–64), Editor-in-chief of *Filmworld* (1964–81); Executive Director of the Academy of Indian Motion Picture Arts and Sciences (1981–84); and from 1984 onwards Editor and Publisher of *Cinema* India-International.

1	Battleship Potemkin/ Bronenosets Potyomkin*
2	Voina i Mir/War and Peace
3	Hiroshima Mon Amour*
4	Fanny and Alexander/ Fanny och Alexander*
5	8½/Otto e Mezzo*
6	The Sacrifice/Sacrificatio*
7	Mephisto
8	Kagemusha
9	The Godfather
10	Gandhi

FIRST MOVIE: *Bronenosets Potyomkin/ Battleship Potemkin* (Eisenstein).
FIRST FILM WALKED OUT OF/
LEAST FAVOURITE MOVIE: Not worth mentioning.

TONY RAYNS
BORN: 1948

Tony Rayns has been an independent filmmaker since his teens. He has directed documentaries on cinema for TV and written screenplays and books on film. He has lectured at the Royal College of Art, London, and been a film festival consultant and consultant to the National Film Archive.

1	Qingmei Zhuma/Tapei Story
2	Haizi Wang/ King of the Children
3	Aienkyo/ Straits of Love and Hate
4	Sans Soleil/Sunless
5	The Scarlet Empress*
6	A Matter of Life and Death/ Stairway to Heaven*
7	Lantou-Ho/Dirty Ho
8	Touch of Evil*
9	Prachachon Nork/ On the Fringe of Society
10	Performance

FIRST MOVIE: In infancy: Disney's *Bambi*; in teens: Anger's *Scorpio Rising*.
FIRST FILM WALKED OUT OF/
LEAST FAVOURITE MOVIE: Assuming you mean film of substance and ambition, Tarkovsky's *Solaris*.
COMMENT: Sometime in the 1970s I began to lose faith in most new American and European cinema . . . Oriental films gave me back the pleasure that I had been missing in Western films.

DAVID ROBINSON
BORN: 1930

David Robinson, who lives in London, was Editor of *Monthly Film Bulletin* (1955–6), Associate Editor of *Sight and Sound* (1955–6) and film critic for the *Financial Times* (1958–73). Since 1973 he has been film critic for *The Times*. He has also been Programme Director for the National Film Theatre (1957–8). His books include *Chaplin: His Life and Art*, *World Cinema*, *Buster Keaton* and *Hollywood in the Twenties*. His list is in chronological order.

Fantomas
The Kid
Our Hospitality
L'Age d'Or/The Golden Age*
Stagecoach*
Ivan the Terrible Parts I and II/ Ivan Groznyi*
Tokyo Story/ Tokyo Monogatari*
If . . .*
L'Enfant Sauvage/ The Wild Child
The Dead

FIRST MOVIE: *Alice in Wonderland* (McLeod, 1932).
FIRST FILM WALKED OUT OF/
LEAST FAVOURITE MOVIE: Can't remember but no one would know the title.

NICK RODDICK
BORN: 1945

Nick Roddick was Films Editor of *Stills* magazine (1982–4) and Editor of *Cinema Papers* (Australia, 1985–6). Since 1986 he has been Deputy Editor, then Editor, of *Screen International* (London).

1	La Règle du Jeu/ The Rules of the Game*
2	The Searchers*
3	Ikiru/Living*
4	The Long Goodbye
5	Als Twee Druppels Water/ Like Two Drops of Water
6	La Dolce Vita*
7	Written on the Wind
8	Finye/The Wind
9	Brief Encounter*
10	Peeping Tom

FIRST MOVIE: *Giant* (Stevens)
FIRST FILM WALKED OUT OF/
LEAST FAVOURITE MOVIE: Memories, thankfully fade. But, in the last decade, *Top Gun*.
COMMENT: I've taken 'favourite' at face value. There are other films I might rate more highly (though none higher than the top three) in terms of their influence, importance, etc. For the record, though, I think *Citizen Kane* (which will undoubtedly figure in your final Top Ten) overrated, both dramatically and cinematically.

JOHN RUSSELL TAYLOR

BORN: 1935

John Russell Taylor, the British film writer, was critic for *The Times* (1962–73) and Professor, Division of Cinema, at the University of Southern California, (1972–8). Since 1983 he has been Editor of *Films and Filming*. His books include *Strangers in Paradise* (1983), *Alec Guinness* (1984) and *Orson Welles* (1986). His list is in no particular order.

Singin' in the Rain*	
Funny Face	
The Hunchback of Notre Dame (1938)	
A Midsummer Night's Dream (1936)	
The Red Shoes	
The Thief of Bagdad*	
Marnie	
Ivan the Terrible Parts I and II/ Ivan Groznyi*	
Kind Hearts and Coronets*	
Bride of Frankenstein	

FIRST MOVIE: *Curly Top* (and several more Shirley Temples, closely followed by Deanna Durbin and Sonja Henie).

FIRST FILM WALKED OUT OF/

LEAST FAVOURITE MOVIE: (Meaningfully at least) *Blue Collar*.

COMMENT: Obviously I like fantasy, glamour, personal vision, style – I'm content to save reality for life – and even there avoid it whenever possible.

CESAR SANTOS FONTENLA

BORN: 1931

Cesar Santos Fontenla is a film critic and lives in Madrid.

1	Singin' in the Rain*
2	Fat City
3	La Règle du Jeu/ The Rules of the Game*
4	The Night of the Hunter
5	Bride of Frankenstein*
6	Battleship Potemkin/ Bronenosets Potyomkin*
7	On the Town
8	Miracolo a Milano/ Miracle in Milan
9	Bienvenido, Mr Marshall
10	Viaggio in Italia/ Voyage to Italy/ The Divorcee of Naples/ The Greatest Love/ Love is the Strongest/ The Lonely Wife

FIRST MOVIE: *Sanders of the River* (Korda).

ANDREW SARRIS

BORN: 1928

Andrew Sarris has been film critic for the New York *Village Voice* since 1940. He is Professor of Film, School of the Arts, Columbia University and author of *The American Cinema, Confessions of a Cultist, The Primal Scream, Politics and Cinema, The John Ford Movie Mystery*, and other works.

1	Madame De .../ The Earrings of Madame De .../ Diamond Earrings*
2	La Règle du Jeu/ The Rules of the Game*
3	Ugetsu Monogatari*
4	Sunrise*
5	Vertigo*
6	The Searchers*
7	The Magnificent Ambersons
8	The Great Dictator*
9	Steamboat Bill, Jr
10	Ordet/The Word*

FIRST MOVIE: William Wellman's *Robin Hood of El Dorado*.

FIRST FILM WALKED OUT OF/

LEAST FAVOURITE MOVIE: I've probably blocked it from my memory.

VECDI SAYAR

BORN: 1950

Vecdi Sayar is Founder/Director of the Ankara Cinematheque; Director of the Turkish Cinematheque; Counsellor on cinema to the Minister of Culture; Founder of the Department of Cinematography; Director of the Committee for International Relations of Turkish Cinema; General Secretary of the Third Balcanic Film Festival and member of various juries. He has been an assistant director and art director on several films and is currently a film critic and Programme Director for the International Istanbul Film Festival.

1	El Angel Exterminador/ The Exterminating Angel*
2	Zéro de Conduite/ Zero for Conduct*
3	Modern Times*
4	Wild Strawberries/ Smultronstället*
5	Morte a Venezia/ Death in Venice
6	Alice in den Stadten/ Alice in the Cities
7	O Thiasos/ The Travelling Players
8	Hiroshima Mon Amour
9	The Servant
10	L'Avventura*

FIRST MOVIE: *The Kid* (Chaplin).

JAY SCOTT
BORN: 1949

Jay Scott was film critic for the *Albuquerque Journal* (1972–5), and *Albertan* (Calgary, 1975–7). Since 1977 he has been film critic for the *Toronto Globe and Mail*. He is the author of *Midnight Matinees: Movies and Their Makers* (1987).

1	The Wizard of Oz*
2	Napoléon*
3	Berlin Alexanderplatz
4	The Magic Flute
5	Ikiru/Living*
6	The Godfather I and II
7	La Notte di San Lorenzo/ The Night of the Shooting Stars
8	The Black Stallion
9	Full Metal Jacket
10	All That Jazz

FIRST MOVIE: *The Teahouse of the August Moon* (Daniel Mann); first to inspire enthusiasm: *Snow White*.

TADEUSZ SOBOELWSKI
BORN: 1947

Tadeusz Soboelwski has contributed reviews, interviews and essays to various Polish film weeklies and monthlies for the past 15 years. He has also contributed essays to books on Cassavetes, Tarkovsky and Wajda.

1	Le Notti di Cabiria/Cabiria/ Nights of Cabiria*
2	Nattvards Gästerna/Winter Light
3	Modern Times*
4	Rosemary's Baby
5	Dersu Uzala
6	Lasky Jedne Plavovlasky/ A Blonde in Love
7	Rekopis Znaleziony w Saragossie/ The Saragossa Manuscript
8	Pociag/Night Train
9	La Nuit Américaine/ Day for Night
10	Meet Me in St Louis*

FIRST MOVIE: *Regained Happiness* (Pudovkine, 1953), the first feature film I ever saw; *Ivan's Childhood* (Tarkovsky), one of my first favourite films.
FIRST FILM WALKED OUT OF/
LEAST FAVOURITE MOVIE: *Oktyabre/October* (Eisenstein).
COMMENT: Film is an art (?) which requires my partnership. I believe – like subjectivists (Berkeley) – that a film shown behind my back, without my presence, does not exist.

SUSAN SONTAG

Susan Sontag, distinguished American woman of letters, writes: 'I've made four feature-length films and written some about film (among other things). I am not a film critic.' Her list is in no particular order.

Tokyo Monogatari/Tokyo Story*
La Règle du Jeu/ The Rules of the Game*
Europa 51
Tengoku to Jigoku/ High and Low
Anjo-ke no Buto-Kai The Ball at the House of Anjo
The Big Parade
Hitler, Ein Film aus Deutschland/ Hitler, A Film from Germany
Ossessione
Jeanne Dielman, 23 Quai du Commerce, 1080 Bruxelles
Prima della Rivoluzione/ Before the Revolution

COMMENT: These are 'favourite' movies – not all of which I necessarily think belong on a 10 'greatest' list.

IVAN STOYANOVICH
BORN: 1930

Ivan Stoyanovich has been a film critic and journalist since 1957. He is Editor-in-chief of the review, *Bulgarian Films*, President of the Film Journalist section in Bulgaria, and the author of many books and articles.

1	8½/Otto e Mezzo*
2	Fanny and Alexander/ Fanny och Alexander*
3	One Flew Over The Cuckoo's Nest*
4	All That Jazz
5	Monanieba/Repentance
6	Le Charme Discret de la Bourgeoisie/ The Discreet Charm of the Bourgeoisie*
7	Mephisto
8	City Lights*
9	Annie Hall
10	Rashomon*

FIRST MOVIE: *Jesse James* (Henry King)
FIRST FILM WALKED OUT OF/
LEAST FAVOURITE MOVIE: Impossible answer.

DAVID STRATTON
BORN: 1939

David Stratton is film critic for *Variety* (Australia), host of *Movie of the Week* and *Cinema Classics* on SBS Network (Australia), co-host of *the Movie Show* (SBS) and an ex-Director of the Sydney Film Festival (1966–83).

1	Singin' in the Rain*
2	Citizen Kane*
3	La Grande Illusion/ Grand Illusion*
4	The Grapes of Wrath
5	Greed*
6	The General*
7	Ikiru/Living*
8	North by Northwest
9	Dr Strangelove
10	Une Femme Mariée/ A Married Woman

FIRST MOVIE: *Duel in the Sun* (Vidor *et al.*)
FIRST FILM WALKED OUT OF/
LEAST FAVOURITE MOVIE: *The Sound of Music* (Wise).
COMMENT: The 'worst' choice was fun: lots to choose from (most recently Stallone in *Over the Top* and the dreaded Spacek/ Bancroft duo in *Night Mother*), but I've settled for *Sound of Music* because singing, dancing or flying nuns always set my teeth on edge, and Julie Andrews was and remains the most loathesomely wholesome heroine in the business.

DAVID SYLVESTER
BORN: 1924

David Sylvester is more commonly known as a writer on art but has written on movies for *Encounter* (London), including the first celebration on Marilyn Monroe to appear in that sort of magazine.' He also wrote for the *New Statesman*, *BBC Comment* and *Harpers and Queen*. His list is in no particular order.

L'Age d'Or/The Golden Age*
Le Charme Discret de la Bourgeoisie/ The Discreet Charm of the Bourgeoisie*
Il Vangelo Secondo Matteo/ The Gospel according to St Matthew
Ai-No Corrida/Empire of the Senses*
Die Büchse der Pandora/ Pandora's Box
Ivan the Terrible Parts I and II/ Ivan Groznyi*
Flesh
The Searchers*
42nd Street
La Bête Humaine

FIRST MOVIE: The first film I recall seeing that impressed me was *Trader Horn* (Van Dyke).
COMMENT: I wanted to include great films of different genres. My list is not so much a mixture of the best and the personal but rather I wanted to include masterpieces of many kinds.

BERTRAND TAVERNIER
BORN: 1941

Bertrand Tavernier is a film critic, director, writer and producer. His most recent films are *Sunday in the Country* and *Round Midnight*. He lives in Paris.

1	La Règle du Jeu/ The Rules of the Game*
2	L'Atalante*
3	I Walked with a Zombie
4	Madame De …/ The Earrings of Madame De …/ Diamond Earrings*
5	Ugetsu Monogatari*
6	The Life and Death of Colonel Blimp
7	Casque d'Or/Golden Marie*
8	The Crowd
9	Sunrise*
10	Fury

FIRST MOVIE: *Gung Ho* (Enright); *Wake of the Red Witch* (Ludwig)
COMMENT: Bertrand Tavernier extended his top 10 to include: *Pursued*; *The Searchers*; *Make Way for Tomorrow*; *Singin' in the Rain*; *Heaven Can Wait* (Lubitsch). He deliberately excluded films made after 1960.

EVAN WILLIAMS
BORN: 1934

Evan Williams has been film critic on the Australian *Voice* (1953–4), *Sydney Morning Herald* (1968–70) and *Australian Playboy* (1979–81). Since 1981 he has been film critic for *The Australian* and since 1987 has served on the ABC-TV panel. He has been a jury member for the Australian Film Institute Awards (199, 1981) and Chairman of the Australian Film Board of Review since 1987. He is also an amateur filmmaker.

1	The Lady Vanishes*
2	The African Queen*
3	It Happened One Night
4	A Matter of Life and Death/ Stairway to Heaven*
5	Rebecca*
6	Hamlet
7	Love Me Tonight
8	Kind Hearts and Coronets*
9	Easter Parade
10	Nashville

FIRST MOVIE: *Three Little Pigs* (Disney, 1937).
FIRST FILM WALKED OUT OF/
LEAST FAVOURITE MOVIE: *History of the World: Part I* (Brooks).
COMMENT: Above are *favourite* films – not necessarily the greatest, the most important, the best, or the most influential – just those that I happen to love!

GINO WIMMER
BORN: 1919

In 1948 Gino Wimmer was location assistant director on Carol Reed's *The Third Man* and a year later assistant director to Reed, Allegret, Hathaway and other directors. Between 1958 and 1968 he was Director of Publicity and Advertising for United Artists in Austria; in 1968 this also included Disney and Rank. Since 1968 he has been film critic for the Vienna *Neue Kronen Zeitung*.

1	Giardino dei Finzi-Contini/ The Garden of the Finzi-Contini
2	Casque d'Or/Golden Marie*
3	Au Revoir les Enfants/ Goodbye Children
4	From Here to Eternity
5	Rashomon*
6	Ran
7	Mr Deeds Goes to Town
8	Orphée
9	Empty Quarter
10	Insignificance

FIRST MOVIE: *Wings* – a silent movie (Wellman, 1927).
FIRST FILM WALKED OUT OF/
LEAST FAVOURITE MOVIE: *Blue Velvet* (Lynch).

DEBORAH YOUNG
BORN: 1952

Deborah Young is film reviewer for *Variety* in Rome.

1	Viridiana*
2	L'Atalante*
3	The Great Dictator*
4	Duck Soup
5	So This Is Paris
6	Madame De .../ The Earrings of Madame De .../ Diamond Earrings*
7	Othello
8	Die Büchse der Pandora/ Pandora's Box
9	Il Conformista/The Conformist
10	Vampyr

FIRST MOVIE: *Zabriskie Point* (Antonioni).
FIRST FILM WALKED OUT OF/
LEAST FAVOURITE MOVIE: *Zoin's Lemma* (Hollis Frampton).
COMMENT: Ten is pure sadism. Picking 100 would have been easier.

EVA ZAORALOVÁ
BORN: 1932

Eva Zaoralová has been film critic for the Prague daily paper *Svobodné Slovo* and for the monthly *Film a Doba* since 1968.

1	Das Kabinett des Dr Caligari/ The Cabinet of Dr Caligari*
2	Un Chien Andalou
3	Les Enfants du Paradis/ Children of Paradise*
4	Battleship Potemkin/ Bronenosets Potyomkin*
5	Bicycle Thieves/ The Bicycle Thief/ Ladri di Biciclette*
6	La Strada/The Road*
7	La Dolce Vita*
8	Fanny and Alexander/ Fanny och Alexander*
9	Blow Up
10	Apocalypse Now

FIRST MOVIE: *Tabu* (Murnau).

KRZYSZTOF ZANUSSI
BORN: 1939

Krzysztof Zanussi is a screenwriter and director who lives in Paris. His list is in approximate chronological order.

Ordet/The Word*
Citizen Kane*
Rashomon*
La Strada*
The Seventh Seal/ Det Sjunde Inseglet*
East of Eden*
Ma Nuit Chez Maud/ My Night with Maud
Jules et Jim*
Le Phantôme de la Liberté/ Phantom of Liberty
Czlowiek z Marmaru/ A Man of Marble

FIRST MOVIE: *La Chartreuse De Parme* (Christian Jaques, 1947).